EMMA MAXWELL

Retirement Planning Made Easy

Contents

Introduction

Retirement isn't just an end; it's a new beginning. Yet, many approach it with uncertainty and anxiety. Consider this: nearly half of Americans haven't calculated how much they'll need in retirement. This isn't just a statistic; it's a wake-up call. It's a reminder that planning for retirement is crucial, no matter where you stand today.

This book is here to empower you. Whether you're just starting or feel late to the game, you can take control of your retirement planning. You can build a future where money worries don't cloud your golden years. This guide is your road map, showing you the steps to build a secure financial future.

Let me introduce myself. I'm Emma, a certified public accountant with over 30 years of experience. I see people every day who struggle with finances. My passion lies in helping them grow their financial knowledge. With this book, I aim to equip you with the tools you need to make informed decisions and achieve financial security.

This book is for those nearing retirement, those starting late, and those over 50 wondering if they can retire comfortably. It addresses the unique challenges you face. It offers strategies to accelerate savings, navigate healthcare costs, and understand when and how to draw on your retirement savings. If you're wondering about social security and when to claim it, I've got that covered too.

What sets this book apart? It simplifies complex financial concepts. You won't find complicated jargon or complex theories here. Instead, you'll get actionable, step-by-step guidance. You'll discover clear, practical advice that can make a real difference. The goal is to make retirement planning accessible, no matter your financial background.

My experience with clients who struggle with finances has taught me so much. I've seen firsthand the impact of financial insecurity. But I've also seen the transformative power of financial education. I'm committed to helping you achieve the peace of mind that comes with being financially prepared.

So, what can you expect from this book? Here are the key takeaways;

- How much money you'll need to retire to cover your cost of living
- What to do if you don't have enough money
- Catch up strategies to boost your retirement account
- Building a healthcare emergency fund
- Potential investment options for your portfolio
- Understanding the Social Security basics
- Preparing for healthcare costs in retirement
- All things estate planning
- Living your best retirement life
- Planning for life when you retire

You'll learn how to assess your current financial situation. You'll discover how much you need to retire comfortably. You'll explore strategies to boost your savings, even if you're starting late. You'll get insights into managing healthcare costs and making the most of social security. By the end of this journey, you'll have a clear plan for a stress-free retirement.

The book is structured logically, starting with the basics and moving on to more advanced topics. Here's a brief overview of the chapters;

1. Building a Strong Foundation
2. Accelerating Your Savings
3. Smart Investment Choices
4. Navigating Social Security
5. Healthcare and Long-Term Care Planning
6. Estate and Legacy Planning

7. Managing Debt and Fixed Income
8. Emotional and Psychological Preparation
9. Future-Proofing Your Retirement
10. Living a Fulfilling Retirement

Each chapter will end with specific, actionable steps you can take to improve your financial situation right away. You'll have a clear path to follow, making it easier to take control of you financial future.

I want to inspire you with optimism and confidence. It's never too late to start planning for a fulfilling retirement. With the right tools and mindset, you can turn financial anxiety into financial freedom. Let this book be your guide to a future filled with possibilities, where your retirement dreams become a reality.

Chapter 1

Building a Strong Foundation

Did you know that the average person spends almost 20 years in retirement? That's two decades filled with experiences, memories, and the freedom to do what you love. Yet, for many, this prospect is overshadowed by the fear of financial insecurity. This chapter aims to transform that fear into confidence by helping you build a solid foundation for your future. It's about laying the groundwork for a retirement that supports your dreams, not hinders them. By understanding your retirement needs, you'll be equipped to create a plan that aligns with your aspirations, ensuring a fulfilling and financially secure retirement.

1.1 Understanding Your Retirement Needs

To begin, could you consider what your ideal retirement looks like? Is it a cozy cabin in the mountains or a beachfront condo? Do you envision days filled with travel or perhaps time spent volunteering at your favorite local charity? Envisioning these details helps clarify what truly matters to you. It's more than just financial security; it's about picturing the life you want to live and identifying the steps needed to achieve it. Reflect on these aspirations and allow them to guide your planning process. You can pinpoint specific needs and desires by visualizing your retirement lifestyle, creating a financial road map tailored to your unique vision.

Common retirement goals often include travel, pursuing hobbies, or engaging in volunteer work. Travel might mean visiting grandchildren across the country or exploring new cultures abroad. Hobbies could range from painting to gardening, offering both relaxation and fulfillment. Volunteering provides a sense of purpose, allowing you to give back to your community. These goals highlight the diverse ways people choose to spend their retirement years. Recognizing your personal priorities within these areas ensures that your plans reflect what's most important to you. By clearly defining your goals, you set the stage for a retirement that aligns with your passions and interests.

Distinguishing between needs and wants is crucial in retirement planning. Needs encompass essential expenses such as housing, healthcare, and basic living costs, whereas wants might involve luxury vacations or high-end purchases. Creating a hierarchical list of retirement expenses helps prioritize these categories, ensuring that your financial resources cover necessities first. Strategies for balancing needs and discretionary spending involve careful budgeting and mindful decision-making. By allocating funds wisely, you maintain a lifestyle that supports your essentials while still allowing room for occasional indulgences. This balance forms the backbone of a sound financial plan, enabling you to enjoy your retirement without compromising security.

Consider potential future scenarios that could impact your retirement. Changes in health, market fluctuations, or unexpected life events can alter your financial landscape. Engaging in scenario planning exercises helps prepare for these possibilities. For instance, envision the effects of a sudden medical expense or a dip in market performance. By anticipating these challenges, you build resilience into your financial plan, ensuring you're equipped to handle unforeseen changes. Factors affecting future retirement needs might include healthcare advancements or shifts in economic conditions. Acknowledging these variables facilitates proactive planning, allowing you to adapt and thrive in a dynamic world.

Self-assessment is a vital tool in aligning your current situation with your retirement vision. Begin by evaluating your readiness through comprehensive checklists that address financial, emotional, and practical aspects. Reflective questions help gauge your priorities, prompting you to consider whether your current trajectory supports your long-term goals. This introspection encourages honest evaluation, revealing areas that may require adjustment. Perhaps you'll find that your savings need a boost, or your investment strategy needs diversification. Whatever the outcome, self-assessment empowers you to take informed action, bridging the gap between where you are and where you want to be.

1.2 Setting Realistic Financial Goals

Setting realistic financial goals is the cornerstone of successful retirement planning. It requires clear, specific objectives that guide your savings and spending habits. The SMART framework—Specific, Measurable, Attainable, Relevant and Time-bound—serves as a reliable method for crafting these goals. For instance, instead of vaguely planning to "save more," aim to "increase retirement savings by 15% over the next year." This goal is specific and measurable, providing a clear target and timeline. By focusing on achievable and relevant goals, you align your efforts with your broader financial aspirations. Consider using goal-setting worksheets to flesh out these details, providing structure and clarity to your planning process. This approach not only motivates you but also keeps you accountable, ensuring each step you take brings you closer to your ultimate retirement vision.

Aligning your financial goals with your retirement timeline is another crucial step. Your expected retirement age and current savings play significant roles in determining how much you need to save and how quickly. For example, if you plan to retire at 67, experts like Fidelity suggest aiming to save 10 times your income by then. Delaying retirement until age 70 might reduce this to eight times, thanks to prolonged growth time for savings and increased Social Security benefits. These general milestones serve as helpful benchmarks, offering a "peg in the sand" to aim for. But for more personalized estimates utilize online retirement calculators, like Boldin to project your growth and adjust your savings plan accordingly. These tools provide a visual representation of your progress, helping you see where you stand and what adjustments are necessary. By setting goals that align with your timeline, you ensure your financial plan is both realistic and achievable.

Life is unpredictable, so incorporating flexibility into your financial goals is essential. Unforeseen events—such as market fluctuations or unexpected expenses—can derail even the most meticulous plans. Flexible financial planning strategies allow you to adapt without losing sight of your objectives. For instance, you might adjust your savings rate temporarily in response to a financial setback, then increase it when circumstances improve. This adaptability ensures your goals remain relevant and attainable, no matter what life throws your way. By building flexibility into your plan, you create a safety net that cushions against uncertainties, helping you maintain momentum toward your retirement targets.

To track and adjust your financial goals efficiently, leverage the power of financial planning tools. Software like Boldin offers comprehensive resources for managing your retirement plan. This platform provides detailed projections, "What if" scenarios, and holistic assessments, helping you see the impacts of different strategies. Boldin is free for the basic version and $120 per year for a more detailed version that gives you multiple what-if scenario plans. Financial planning apps such as YNAB (You Need a Budget) or Empower offer user-friendly interfaces for tracking expenses and income, making it easier to stay on top of your finances. These tools not only simplify the tracking process by linking with your bank accounts but also provide valuable insights, highlighting areas for improvement and celebrating your progress. By utilizing these resources, you gain control over your financial journey, ensuring your goals evolve alongside your changing circumstances. I go into this in great depth in my first book **Financial Freedom Made Easy: Step-by-Step Guide to Eliminate Debt, Create a Financial Plan, and Provide Financial Security for You and Your Family,** so I won't spend too much time on it here.

1.3 Demystifying Retirement Jargon

Retirement planning often feels like venturing into a foreign land where everyone speaks a language you don't understand. Terms like 401(k), IRA, and annuity are tossed around, leaving many bewildered and frustrated. Let's break down these complex terms, simplifying them to empower you in making informed decisions. A 401(k) is an employer-sponsored retirement savings plan allowing tax-deductible and pre-tax employee contributions. Think of it as a special savings account where your money grows tax-free until you withdraw it in retirement. An IRA, or Individual Retirement Account, is another type of savings vehicle. It offers tax advantages, with contributions either being tax-deferred (Traditional IRA) or made with after-tax dollars (Roth IRA). An annuity, on the other hand, involves payments to an insurance company in exchange for a series of payments during retirement. By understanding these definitions, you eliminate confusion and gain confidence in your financial planning.

Understanding these terms is not just about sounding smart at your next dinner party; it's crucial for effective retirement planning. For instance, knowing the difference between a Traditional and a Roth IRA can significantly impact your tax strategy. A Traditional IRA allows you to defer taxes on contributions until withdrawal, which could be beneficial if you expect to be in a lower tax bracket in retirement. In contrast, a Roth IRA involves paying taxes upfront, but earnings and withdrawals are tax-free. Contextual examples of jargon in financial planning highlight why these distinctions matter. When deciding on investment options, knowing what a diversified portfolio entails ensures you're spreading risk across various asset classes, not putting all your eggs in one basket. This understanding aids in making decisions that align with your retirement goals and risk tolerance.

Analogies and real-life examples can further illuminate complex concepts. Picture a 401(k) as a garden. You plant seeds (your contributions) and nurture them over time. The employer's matching contributions act like fertilizer, boosting growth. As years pass, your garden flourishes, providing a bountiful harvest at retirement. In real life, consider someone who carefully monitored their investment mix, maintaining a balanced portfolio through market ups and downs. This strategy allowed them to weather financial storms, ensuring stability in retirement. Such analogies and scenarios bring clarity, transforming abstract terms into relatable concepts that resonate with everyday experiences.

1.4 Assessing Your Current Financial Situation

The first step in assessing your financial situation is conducting a detailed financial inventory. This involves taking stock of all your assets, liabilities, and income streams. If you've read my first book you would have done this already but if you haven't let's do that now. Imagine your finances as a puzzle, each piece representing a different element of your financial life. Start by listing your assets—these are the pieces that add value to your overall picture. Include properties, savings accounts, investments, and any other valuable possessions. Next, account for your liabilities—these are the debts that subtract from your total worth, such as mortgages, loans, and credit card balances. Finally, outline your income streams, including salaries, pensions, or any other sources of regular income. By laying out each piece clearly, you gain a comprehensive view of your financial landscape, making it easier to identify strengths and weaknesses. Use a financial inventory template or use a similar format to below to organize this information systematically, ensuring no detail is overlooked.

As you compile your inventory, consider what your living expenses will be when you retire. We'll do this in more detail in Chapter 7 but you can come back and fill in this template then if you like. It's crucial to differentiate between current expenses and those you'll face in retirement. While some costs, like commuting, may decrease, others, such as healthcare, may rise. This exercise provides a clearer picture of your financial needs, helping you plan accordingly. To aid in this process, I've included a template below where you can crunch the numbers for yourself. By estimating your future expenses, you can better understand the financial adjustments required to maintain your desired lifestyle.

Net Worth Template

Assets $ Value
   Principal Place of Residence
   Investment Property
   Savings Account
   Checking Account
   Personal Investments
   Retirement Account
   Share Account

Sellable Assets
   Car
   Jewelry
   Boat
   Other
   Total Assets

Liabilities
   Mortgage on Principal Place of Residence
   Mortgage on Investment Property
   Credit card Debt
   Car Loans
   Charge Cards
   Other Liabilities
   Total Liabilities

Net Worth (Assets minus Liabilities)

Income & Expenses Template
Now In Retirement

Income
You

Your spouse

Pension

Social Security

Rental Income

Investment Income

Other

Total Income

Expenses
Now In Retirement
Mortgage

Utilities

Property taxes

Strata/HOA fees

Groceries

Children costs

Medical

Insurance

Beauty

Alcohol

Entertainment

Clothing

Vacations

Presents

Investment property expenses

Car running costs

Other

Total Expenses

Net Income/Profit

Once you've completed your template, it's time to evaluate your savings and investments. This involves analyzing your existing savings plans and investment portfolios to determine their current value and potential for growth. Assess whether your retirement savings are on track to meet your retirement goals. Consider factors such as your current savings rate, investment returns, and any employer contributions. You should be able to access this on the online retirement portal for who you have your retirement account with. Evaluate your investment portfolio to ensure it aligns with your risk tolerance and financial objectives. Are your assets diversified enough to weather market fluctuations? Are your investments performing as expected? To find this out look at your last quarter/yearly financial summary of your retirement account which will show you where your portfolio is invested, what plan it is and what % return it has been achieving as well as the fees you're being charged. You should be aiming for a minimum of 7% return as you build towards retirement whilst still working. By answering these questions, you can identify areas for improvement and ensure your savings are working effectively for you.

Log in to the free version of Boldin, create an account and fill in the information they request. It will then calculate the Social Security you're expected to earn at what age and predict the retirement balance you need for the retirement age you enter. On the overview page it has a yearly graph that shows how your retirement balance grows over time; the beauty of compounding interest. It then says what your % chance of success in funding your retirement and then underneath that it calculates what your net worth now and in retirement. If this % is not 75% or greater we have work to do.

Identifying financial gaps and opportunities is the next step. Perhaps you need to increase your savings rate, adjust your investment strategy, or reconsider your retirement age. Each gap represents an opportunity for optimization. Make sure you have your employer matching your retirement contributions as this is basically free money. For instance, if you're behind on savings, consider boosting your contributions or exploring new investment avenues. Alternatively, if your retirement age feels unrealistic, evaluate the benefits of working a few more years to enhance your financial security. If your retirement account is delivering less than 5% you need to consider changing this whilst you're still working to increase the return. The power of compounding is your friend as it will reinvest what you've earned this year and get another year's return on it again and again. You need to be comfortable with this change in risk strategy. Don't go investing your retirement account into crypto, but if you can move from say 100% bonds to a mix of blue-chip shares, international shares, real estate and bonds you will likely get a higher return. Often times the fund you are with will have different fund types that you can choose from based on the year you will retire and you can check their performance over time to see if they have performed well. It should just be a simple online change in your account to make this happen. By identifying these gaps, you highlight areas for targeted action, paving the way for financial improvement.

Prioritizing actions for improvement involves taking actionable steps to address the gaps identified. Start by listing each gap and determining which areas need immediate attention. Perhaps paying off high-interest debt should take precedence, or maybe maximizing employer contributions to your retirement plan is more urgent. By prioritizing these actions, you create a clear road map for enhancing your financial readiness. Develop a timeline for implementing these changes, setting realistic deadlines for each task. This structured approach ensures that improvements are manageable and sustainable, leading to a stronger financial foundation. As you work through this process, you'll find that each step brings you closer to achieving the financial security and peace of mind you desire for retirement.

1.5 Prioritizing Your Retirement Goals

In retirement planning, prioritizing goals is crucial. Picture your goals as a ladder, each rung representing a different priority. Begin by ranking these goals based on personal values and financial impact. For some, ensuring a comfortable home might top the list, while others may prioritize traveling the world or supporting their grandchildren's education. Ranking exercises can help clarify which goals are most important. Consider factors such as immediate necessity, emotional fulfillment, and potential financial return. This process not only organizes your objectives but also provides a clear direction, ensuring your resources align with your most cherished aspirations.

Balancing short-term and long-term objectives requires a keen understanding of both immediate financial needs and future aspirations. It's akin to maintaining a seesaw, where one side represents your immediate wants, and the other your long-term dreams. Short-term decisions, such as purchasing a new car or taking a spontaneous vacation, should always consider their impact on long-term financial security. The power of compounding underscores this balance. Small, consistent investments today can yield significant growth over time, reinforcing the importance of planning for the future. By carefully weighing each financial decision, you create a plan that supports both your present enjoyment and future stability.

Regularly revisiting and adjusting priorities is vital. Life's ever-changing nature means that what matters today might shift tomorrow. Regular reassessment keeps your goals relevant, helping you adapt to new circumstances. Tips for reassessment include setting aside time each year to review your financial plan, ensuring it aligns with current life stages and market conditions. Tools like Empower and You Need a Budget (YNAB) can simplify this process, offering reminders and tracking progress. These platforms allow you to tweak goals effortlessly, ensuring your plan remains dynamic and responsive. By embracing flexibility, you prepare for life's twists and turns, maintaining a steady course toward your retirement dreams.

Lifestyle preferences play a significant role in shaping retirement goals.

Some envision a quiet life in the countryside, while others crave the vibrancy of city living. These choices influence financial planning, dictating expenses and savings strategies. For instance, a preference for urban life may require budgeting for higher living costs, while those seeking a rural retreat might focus on property investments. Lifestyle-driven priorities ensure your financial plan reflects your unique desires, making retirement not just a phase, but a fulfilling chapter of life. To aid in this, consider engaging in an exercise to crunch the numbers for yourself, evaluating how your lifestyle choices impact your financial needs.

As you navigate this planning process, remember that retirement isn't solely about finances. It's about crafting a life that resonates with your passions and values. By prioritizing your goals thoughtfully, balancing short-term desires with long-term ambitions, and integrating lifestyle preferences, you create a road map tailored to your vision. This proactive approach transforms retirement planning from a daunting task to an empowering endeavor, opening doors to a future rich with opportunity and satisfaction.

Now don't freak out if the number you created for your retirement savings goal is far from where it is now and your Boldin success rate is low. That's why you bought this book so we can make it better.

Don't move on to the next chapter without doing the following;

1. Calculate your net worth
2. Calculate your income and expenses. You can use the template provided or create an account with Empower or You Need a Budget. Empower lets you link your accounts so you can log in and see these updated real time
3. Create a Boldin Account. Enter the income and expenses from the information in 1 & 2
4. Do you need to change your retirement contribution to get your full employer match? Don't wait, do this now!
5. Do you need to change your investment strategy in your online retirement account? Check current fund performance and adjust accordingly

6. Sit down with your partner and plan your ideal retirement life. Where will you live? How much will it cost? And when will you retire?

Chapter 2

Accelerating Your Savings

Imagine preparing for a journey without knowing your destination or the resources you'll need along the way. Many people nearing retirement feel this uncertainty, especially if they find themselves starting the planning process later in life. The good news is that it's never too late to enhance your retirement savings, and there are effective strategies to do so. This chapter is about acceleration—moving your savings into high gear, even if you're beginning from a modest starting point. Whether you're just shy of retirement age or playing catch-up, there are steps you can take to boost your financial preparedness. Let's explore how.

2.1 Maximizing Catch-Up Contributions

As you approach the age of 50, an opportunity opens up to enhance your retirement savings through catch-up contributions. These are additional contributions allowed by the IRS to certain retirement plans, designed specifically for those who recognize the need to amp up their savings as they near retirement. If you're 50 or older by the end of the calendar year, you can make these contributions to plans like 401(k), 403(b), and governmental

457(b). For 2023 and 2024, the catch-up limit is $7,500, a figure that can significantly bolster your retirement kitty. This is particularly beneficial if you've fallen behind in your savings and need a financial boost to ensure a comfortable retirement. However, remember that these contributions only come into play once your regular contributions exceed the annual limit, which is $23,500 for 2024. In 2025 these catch up contributions will grow to $11,250 for those aged 60-63. For those using SIMPLE IRA or SIMPLE 401(k) plans, the catch-up contribution is capped at $3,500.

To make the most of catch-up contributions, start by reallocating discretionary income towards your retirement accounts. Examine your monthly budget, identify areas where you can cut back, and redirect those funds into your retirement savings. For instance, reducing dining out or trimming entertainment expenses can free up significant amounts to contribute. Automating your contributions can be a game-changer. Set up automatic transfers from your checking account to your retirement fund. This ensures consistency and helps you avoid the temptation to spend. By making savings a non-negotiable part of your financial routine, you create a disciplined approach that supports your long-term goals. These changes don't have to be forever, but a one off top up can make a difference over the long term. I always advise people that when they get their annual wage increase or bonus, if they can afford to, put it into retirement savings.

Optimizing contributions across different accounts is another crucial strategy. Compare the contribution limits and benefits of accounts such as 401(k) and IRAs. While 401(k) plans offer higher contribution limits, IRAs provide valuable tax advantages, especially if you're eligible for a Roth IRA. Consider a strategic allocation between pre-tax contributions, which lower your taxable income now, and Roth contributions, which allow for tax-free withdrawals later. This balance can provide a tax-efficient strategy that maximizes growth and flexibility in retirement. Evaluate your current retirement accounts and decide where additional contributions will have the most impact, aligning with both your tax strategy and retirement goals. You can google the contribution limits, contact your HR department or contact a financial advisor.

Regularly reviewing your contributions is vital to stay on track. Use tools to monitor your progress, ensuring your contributions are on pace with your retirement timeline. Financial apps like Empower and YNAB and spreadsheets can help track your savings and highlight areas for adjustment. As your financial situation changes—perhaps due to a raise, a change in expenses, or a shift in retirement goals—adjust your contributions accordingly. If you receive a salary increase, consider boosting your retirement contributions proportionally. This approach not only leverages your increased income but also accelerates your path to financial security. Adjustments to your portfolio may also be necessary, ensuring your investments align with your risk tolerance and market conditions. Regular rebalancing of your portfolio can help maintain your desired asset allocation, optimizing growth while managing risk.

Exercise: Maximizing Your Contributions

Take a moment to evaluate your current savings strategy. Use the checklist below to assess and maximize your contributions:

- **Review Current Contributions**: Are you maximizing your regular and catch-up contributions?
- **Analyze Discretionary Spending**: Identify areas to cut back and redirect funds to savings.
- **Set Up Automation**: Have you automated your contributions for consistency?
- **Adjust for Changes**: Have you adjusted contributions based on recent financial changes or goals?
- **Revisit Portfolio**: Are your investments aligned with your risk tolerance and retirement timeline? What % return has it achieved over the last 5 years and how does it compare to other funds over the same period?

This exercise is designed to provide a clear picture of where you stand and what actions you can take to enhance your savings. Implementing these strategies

RETIREMENT PLANNING MADE EASY

can significantly impact your financial readiness for retirement, ensuring you're well-prepared for this next chapter.

2.2 Leveraging Employer Retirement Plans

When considering your employer's retirement plan, it's crucial to understand the specifics of what they offer. Most companies provide plans like 401(k)s or 403(b)s, which serve as powerful tools for building your nest egg. These plans often come with the option of employer matching contributions, which can significantly amplify your savings. Think of employer matching as free money added to your retirement account, boosting your potential returns without any additional effort on your part. For example, if your employer matches 50% of your contributions up to 6% of your salary, contributing at least 6% ensures you receive the full match. This scenario illustrates the potential missed opportunity if you contribute less and don't take full advantage of the match. Understanding these details helps you make informed decisions that maximize the benefits of your employer's plan.

To fully utilize employer matching, you need to ensure you're contributing enough to receive the complete match. It's surprising how many employees inadvertently leave money on the table by not maximizing their contributions. Consider a scenario where an employee contributes only 3% of their salary, while their employer offers a match up to 6%. In this case, they're missing out on an additional 3% that could have compounded over time. To avoid this, take the necessary steps to align your contributions with the maximum matching limit. Review your plan's terms and adjust your contributions accordingly. If you're unsure what the maximum match is, consult your HR department or plan administrator. By ensuring you contribute enough to receive the full match, you significantly enhance your retirement savings potential.

Increasing your participation in employer retirement plans often requires strategic planning. One effective technique is utilizing automatic escalation features, which gradually increase your contribution rate over time. This feature allows you to start with a manageable percentage and incrementally boost it, typically annually, until you reach your desired contribution level. This gradual increase can make the process less daunting, allowing you to adjust to the higher savings rate without feeling the immediate financial impact. Additionally, early enrollment in new plans can have substantial long-term benefits. By starting to save as soon as you're eligible, you take full advantage of compounding interest, allowing your money more time to grow. This early start can make a significant difference in the overall amount you save by retirement.

Reviewing and optimizing your plan allocations is another crucial aspect of leveraging employer retirement plans. Within your 401(k), diversification is key to managing risk and maximizing returns. Diversification involves spreading your investments across various asset classes, such as stocks, bonds, and cash equivalents, to reduce risk exposure. This strategy helps protect your portfolio from market volatility, ensuring that not all your investments are affected by a downturn in one sector. Rebalancing your portfolio regularly is also essential. This involves adjusting your asset mix to align with your retirement goals and risk tolerance. For example, as you near retirement, you may want to shift towards more conservative investments to preserve your capital. Changing funds within your plan may also be necessary if current funds are under performing. By staying actively involved in managing your retirement plan, you ensure it continues to meet your evolving needs and objectives. You should be able to do all these changes in your retirement funds online portal.

As you consider these strategies, remember that your employer's retirement plan is more than just a savings vehicle; it's a cornerstone of your retirement strategy. By fully understanding the options available, maximizing matching contributions, and optimizing your investment allocations, you can significantly enhance your financial security in retirement. Take the time to review your plan regularly and make adjustments as needed, ensuring it aligns with your changing circumstances and goals. By leveraging these opportunities, you position yourself for a more secure and comfortable retirement.

2.3 Exploring Alternative Income Streams

Retirement doesn't have to mean the end of income generation. Some people don't want to stop work and if that's you then that is 100% fine. In fact, exploring alternative income streams can be a strategic way to bolster your retirement savings. One popular option is freelancing or consulting based on skills you've honed over your career. Perhaps you have a knack for writing, teaching, or providing specialized advice. These are valuable skills that can be monetized without the commitment of a full-time job. For instance, you could offer consultancy services in your field or write articles for industry publications. This not only supplements your income but also keeps you mentally engaged and connected to the professional world. Additionally, monetizing hobbies and passions can be a rewarding way to generate income. Whether it's crafting, photography, or woodworking, turning a beloved pastime into a side business can provide both financial and personal satisfaction.

Assessing the feasibility of side hustles requires careful evaluation of potential income and time investment. Consider the story of Jane, a retired teacher who started tutoring students online. She began with just a few hours a week, gradually building a client base that provided a steady income stream. Her success came from leveraging her existing skills and setting realistic expectations about her availability. Balancing a side job with retirement can be challenging, so effective time management is crucial. Develop a schedule that allows you to enjoy leisure time while dedicating specific hours to your venture. Be mindful of the risk associated with starting a business in retirement. There's a chance that the initial investment of time and resources might not yield the expected returns. It's vital to enter this endeavor with a clear understanding of these risks, ensuring you're not jeopardizing your financial security.

For those seeking less active involvement, passive income streams offer an appealing alternative. Real estate rental investments are a common choice, providing regular income with the potential for property appreciation over time. Owning rental properties requires upfront effort in terms of acquisition and management, but once established, they can generate a steady income flow. Also they can be managed by a property manager to keep it stress free for you. Alternatively, consider dividend-paying stocks, which offer income through company earnings distributed to shareholders. This option allows you to benefit from market growth while receiving periodic income. Both of these avenues require careful research and consideration of market conditions, but they can significantly enhance your financial portfolio without the need for constant oversight.

Integrating additional income into your savings strategy is the next step. Direct deposit setups can automatically channel your side income into retirement accounts, ensuring that extra funds are used wisely. You could consider this or use this money to live on whilst not drawing down as much from your retirement accounts. This automated process reduces the temptation to spend the money elsewhere, reinforcing a disciplined savings approach. Adjusting your budget to prioritize savings contributions ensures that any additional income is effectively utilized. Allocate a portion of your side income to cover immediate expenses, then direct the remaining funds toward boosting your retirement savings. This methodical approach not only enhances your financial security but also instills a sense of achievement as you see your savings grow.

Reflection Section: Assess Your Income Potential

Take a moment to reflect on your skills, passions, and how they could translate into additional income streams. Consider the following questions:

- What skills or expertise do you possess that could be monetized?
- Are there hobbies or interests you could turn into a profitable venture?
- How much time are you willing to dedicate to a side hustle? Balance this with how much you want to travel or do other things
- What are the potential risks and rewards associated with your chosen income stream?

- How can you ensure that any additional income directly benefits your retirement savings?

Use these reflections to craft a plan that leverages your unique talents, ensuring a financially secure and personally fulfilling retirement.

2.4 Reducing Expenses to Boost Savings

Faced with the reality of retirement expenses and the potential gap in savings, many find themselves questioning their financial preparedness. Conducting a thorough expense review is a practical first step in identifying areas where savings can be bolstered. Start by tracking your spending over a month or two using tools and apps designed for this purpose—platforms like Empower or YNAB offer straightforward solutions. I go into this in great detail in my first book **Financial Freedom Made Easy**. Categorize your expenses into essential and discretionary, highlighting areas like dining out, entertainment, and subscription services. These categories often contain hidden opportunities for savings. Once tracked, examine your spending patterns critically. Is that daily coffee run a necessity, or could it be an occasional treat? By pinpointing areas of excess, you create a road map for financial efficiency. Recognizing these patterns not only reveals where you might be overspending but also opens the door to making meaningful adjustments that can significantly impact your financial future.

Implementing cost-saving measures doesn't mean sacrificing quality of life. It's about making smart choices that enhance your financial health without feeling deprived. Start by tackling utility bills; simple actions like unplugging electronics when not in use, using energy-efficient appliances, and adjusting your thermostat can lead to noticeable savings. When it comes to groceries and dining, consider meal planning and bulk buying to reduce costs. Planning meals weekly can help avoid impulse purchases and reliance on takeout. Dining at home doesn't have to be a chore; it can be an opportunity to explore new recipes and enjoy healthier options. Furthermore, conduct a subscription audit. Those monthly charges for streaming services, magazines, or gym memberships can add up. Evaluate which ones you truly use and cancel the rest or use them on and off each month. This approach ensures that your money is spent on what genuinely adds value to your life, freeing up funds for your retirement savings.

Adopting a frugal mindset is key to transforming your financial habits. It begins with mindfulness, a practice that involves being aware of your spending tendencies and examining the motivations behind them. Are purchases driven by need, or are they a response to emotional triggers? Practicing mindfulness can help you become more deliberate in your spending decisions. Techniques for resisting impulse purchases include creating a mandatory waiting period before making non-essential purchases and focusing on long-term goals over immediate gratification. Visualizing your retirement goals can serve as a powerful motivator to resist the allure of unnecessary spending. By cultivating this mindset, you shift from impulsive to intentional spending, ensuring that your financial choices align with your broader objectives.

Channeling the savings from reduced expenses into your retirement fund is the next logical step. Set up automatic transfers from your checking account to your retirement accounts, ensuring that the money saved is immediately put to work or get your HR department to deduct it from your wage/salary. This automation removes the temptation to spend and reinforces a disciplined saving habit. Establishing incremental savings goals based on your reduced expenses can provide tangible milestones to celebrate, reinforcing positive financial behavior. The power of compounding further amplifies these efforts. By investing savings, even modest amounts, into retirement accounts, you harness the growth potential of your contributions over time. This approach not only accelerates your savings but also builds momentum towards a financially secure retirement.

Reflection Section: Implementing a Frugal Mindset

Take a moment to reflect on your current spending habits and how they align with your retirement goals. Consider the following questions:

- What areas of spending could be reduced without affecting your quality of life?
- How can you incorporate mindfulness into your financial decisions?
- Are there specific impulse purchases you can eliminate?
- How might you redirect these savings to enhance your financial future?
- What long-term goals can motivate you to maintain a frugal mindset?

As you ponder these questions, remember that every dollar saved today has the potential to grow, bringing you closer to the retirement lifestyle you envision.

In summary, reducing expenses and adopting a frugal mindset can significantly enhance your retirement savings. By diligently reviewing your spending, implementing cost-saving measures, and redirecting the savings into your retirement accounts, you create a solid financial foundation. As we move forward, the next chapter will explore smart investment choices to further strengthen your retirement plan.

Don't move on to the next chapter without doing the following;

1. Do the exercise on maximizing your contribution
2. Do the exercise on income potential in retirement
3. If you haven't already done it, list out your income and expenses. If your expenses are too big where can you pair back and reduce costs. Implement these immediately to see quick wins and gain momentum

Chapter 3

Smart Investment Choices

Imagine standing at the crossroads of your financial future, holding the power to mold it through the choices you make today. Investing wisely isn't just about growing your money; it's about ensuring stability and security in the years to come. As you approach retirement, these decisions become even more critical. How do you navigate the complex world of investments to create a portfolio that not only withstands market fluctuations but also aligns with your financial goals? The key lies in crafting a diversified portfolio, a strategy that spreads risk and enhances stability, ensuring your investments are both resilient and rewarding.

Diversification is more than a buzzword; it's a fundamental principle that reduces risk and enhances stability within your portfolio. By spreading your investments across various asset classes, you mitigate the risk associated with any single investment's poor performance. Think of it as not putting all your eggs in one basket, where if one basket falls, the others remain intact. Asset allocation plays a crucial role in this strategy, as it involves determining the right mix of stocks, bonds, real estate, and commodities to match your risk tolerance and financial goals. By balancing these components, you create a portfolio that's designed to weather financial storms, maintaining equilibrium even when markets fluctuate. Decreased volatility is one of the primary benefits of diversification, as it smooths out the highs and lows of market movements, providing a more consistent growth trajectory. In your retirement account, you can achieve this by allocating your investments across different asset classes, each contributing to a well-rounded and stable portfolio.

Most retirement accounts offer you some form of choice of what you invest in. You can either pick a portfolio that is the year you will retire which will be more aggressive in your 30s and 40s and get more conservative in your 50s and 60s. These are great for people that don't know a lot about investing. Then depending on what fund you're with, you may be able to choose your own investment options, including individual shares. If you don't know a lot about investing just browse your funds different options and look at past performance. Whilst it's not an indicator of future performance, it will show you what % returns they've been getting across different diversified portfolios. If you decide to switch from what you're currently in, it should be an easy switch online. It also doesn't have to be forever, check back in each quarter and see how it's progressing and you can always switch again.

To develop a diversified portfolio, it's important to identify the key asset classes and understand their roles. Stocks offer the potential for high returns and growth, making them an essential component for those seeking to outpace inflation. Bonds, on the other hand, provide steady income and are generally less volatile than stocks, offering a cushion during market downturns. They are lower returns, around 2% per annum so you would probably only have a small % of your fund made up of bonds until you're older. Real estate investments add another layer of diversification, as they often move independently of stock and bond markets, providing a hedge against inflation. Commodities, such as gold or oil, can further diversify your portfolio, acting as a safeguard against economic uncertainty. A well-balanced portfolio includes a mix of these asset classes, tailored to your financial objectives and risk tolerance. Incorporating both domestic and international investments can also enhance diversification, as global markets may react differently to economic events, spreading risk even further.

Crafting a personalized diversification strategy means tailoring your portfolio to align with your unique financial goals and risk appetite. Assessing your individual risk tolerance is a crucial step in this process. Consider your comfort level with market fluctuations and potential losses, as well as your time horizon for investing. Tools like the Vanguard Investor Questionnaire can help you gauge your risk profile, providing recommendations for asset allocation based on your responses. You should re-do this questionnaire each year to see if your risk profile has changed, when you review your funds performance. Sample diversified portfolio models offer a starting point, illustrating how different allocations might look based on varying risk levels. For instance, a moderate-risk portfolio might consist of 60% stocks, 35% bonds, and 5% cash, while a more conservative approach could lean towards 40% stocks, 50% bonds, and 10% cash. Once you retire, it's essential to re-evaluate whether to maintain the same funds you had while working or adjust your allocations to reflect your new income needs and risk tolerance.

Regularly rebalancing your portfolio is vital to maintaining your target asset allocation and ensuring your investments continue to align with your goals. Over time, market movements can cause your asset mix to deviate from your original plan, potentially increasing risk exposure. Scheduled rebalancing involves reviewing and adjusting your portfolio at predetermined intervals, such as annually or semi-annually, to realign with your desired allocation. Event-driven rebalancing, on the other hand, occurs in response to significant market shifts or life changes. Automatic rebalancing features offered by platforms like Vanguard's Digital Advisor® provide a convenient solution, automatically adjusting your portfolio to maintain balance without requiring constant oversight. By utilizing these methods, you uphold the integrity of your investment strategy, ensuring it remains effective and aligned with your evolving financial landscape. Most funds would rebalance as they buy new stocks so you don't need to worry too much about this unless you're actively managing your own portfolio.

Reflection Section: Diversification Check

Consider your current investment strategy and how diversification plays a role. Reflect on the following:

- Do you understand the balance between stocks, bonds, and other asset classes in your portfolio?
- How comfortable are you with your current level of risk?
- Have you incorporated both domestic and international investments?
- When was the last time you rebalanced your portfolio, and is it aligned with your retirement goals?
- Can you leverage automatic rebalancing tools to simplify this process?

By reflecting on these questions, you ensure your investments are diversified, stable, and tailored to your retirement objectives.

3.1 Understanding Risk and Reward

Every investment decision you make comes with two intertwined elements: risk and reward. These are the yin and yang of investing, constantly balancing each other. Risk involves the chance that your investments might not perform as expected. It can lead to losses, but it's also what makes investing exciting, as it opens the door to potential rewards. Reward, on the other hand, is the return or profit you earn from your investments. The risk–return trade off is a fundamental concept; higher potential returns usually come with higher risk. For example, stocks are often seen as high-risk but can offer significant growth, while government bonds are lower-risk and provide steady, albeit modest, returns. Understanding this trade off is crucial as you plan your investment strategy, helping you align your choices with your comfort level and financial goals.

To assess your personal risk tolerance, it's important to start by under-standing how comfortable you are with the ups and downs of investing. Risk tolerance questionnaires, like those offered by Vanguard, can be incredibly useful tools. They help gauge your emotional and financial ability to handle investment fluctuations. Questions often explore your reaction to market volatility and past experiences with financial loss. Psychological factors also play a role; some individuals are naturally more risk-averse, while others may thrive on the excitement of potential gains. Your current financial situation, future goals, age and how you perceive risk all contribute to forming a clear picture of your risk tolerance. Recognizing these elements allows you to make informed decisions, ensuring your investment strategy aligns with both your financial objectives and emotional comfort.

Once you've assessed your risk tolerance, utilizing risk management strategies can help mitigate potential downsides while pursuing your desired returns. Stop-loss orders in stock trading are one such tool, automatically selling a stock if its price falls to a certain level. This can protect you from significant losses in volatile markets. Hedging strategies, such as options or futures contracts, provide another layer of security, allowing you to offset potential losses in one investment with gains in another. You only need to be actively involved in stop losses or hedging if you are managing your portfolio yourself, otherwise your fund manager manages this all for you. As your risk profile changes, whether due to a shift in financial goals or life circumstances, you'll need to adjust your retirement account fund accordingly. This might involve moving funds from more aggressive investments to safer ones, ensuring that your portfolio remains aligned with your evolving risk tolerance. By implementing these strategies, you create a robust framework that safeguards your investments, allowing you to pursue growth with confidence.

Aligning your investment choices with your risk tolerance is vital for maintaining a balanced and effective portfolio. This means selecting investments that match your risk profile, ensuring you're neither too exposed nor overly conservative. For instance, if you have a low-risk tolerance, a portfolio heavy in bonds and cash might suit you, whereas a higher-risk tolerance could lead to a mix of stocks and real estate. Portfolio adjustments based on risk tolerance are sometimes necessary. If you find that market volatility is causing undue stress or if your financial goals shift, consider rebalancing your portfolio to reflect these changes. Look to real-life case studies of risk-aligned investment strategies for inspiration. For example, a retiree who initially held a stock-heavy portfolio might gradually shift to income-generating bonds as they approach retirement, prioritizing stability over growth. Such adjustments ensure that your investments continue to support your long-term objectives while respecting your personal comfort with risk.

You can actively change your investment option within your retirement account. I suggest a review once a year after you receive your annual statement and go online and see how your fund has performed compared to other funds within your retirement account. It will have the risk profile against each fund and what makes up the mix of that fund. Make an educated decision based on your risk profile, past performance and your stage in life.

3.2 Selecting the Right Investment Vehicles

When you set out to build a robust investment portfolio, the choices available can seem overwhelming. Yet, understanding the different types of investment vehicles is a crucial step in crafting a strategy that aligns with your retirement goals. Mutual funds, for instance, are pooled investment vehicles that allow you to invest in a diversified selection of stocks and bonds, managed by professional fund managers. They offer the advantage of diversification and professional management but often come with higher fees. Exchange-traded funds (ETFs) are similar but trade like individual stocks on an exchange, generally offering lower expense ratios and greater flexibility. Individual stocks represent ownership in a specific company, allowing for potentially high returns but also carrying higher risk. Bonds, on the other hand, are debt instruments where you lend money to an issuer in exchange for periodic interest payments and eventual return of principal. They tend to be more stable than stocks but offer lower returns. Each of these vehicles has its advantages and disadvantages, and the key is to understand how they fit into your overall financial plan.

Investment costs and fees can significantly impact your returns, so it's essential to evaluate them carefully. Expense ratios, which are annual fees expressed as a percentage of the fund's average assets, can erode your returns over time, particularly for mutual funds and ETFs. A seemingly small difference in expense ratios can compound over the years, diminishing your nest egg. Transaction fees, often associated with buying and selling stocks, and hidden costs such as management fees, can further eat into your profits. To minimize these costs, consider low-cost index funds or ETFs that track market indices with lower expense ratios. Also, be aware of the fee structures of your investments and seek transparency from financial advisors, ensuring you understand the true cost of managing your portfolio. This should be transparent in the annual performance statement you receive each year.

Tax implications of your investments can also have a profound effect on your retirement savings. Tax-deferred accounts, like traditional IRAs and 401(k)s, allow you to postpone taxes on your contributions and earnings until you withdraw them in retirement. This can be beneficial if you expect to be in a lower tax bracket when you retire. Taxable accounts, however, require you to pay taxes on dividends and capital gains annually, which can reduce your overall returns. Strategies like tax-loss harvesting can help offset gains by selling securities at a loss to reduce your taxable income. This approach requires careful planning but can enhance tax efficiency, preserving more of your hard-earned wealth. Again this is for people managing their own fund and should only be done if you think the security you're selling wouldn't improve over time. If you're with a managed fund you won't need to worry about this.

Selecting investments that align with your retirement goals involves matching your choices to both short-term and long-term objectives. Short-term goals might include generating income to cover daily expenses, while long-term goals focus on growth to outpace inflation. Goal-driven investment portfolios are tailored to address these needs, balancing risk and reward in line with your personal circumstances and age. For instance, if you're nearing retirement, you may prioritize income-producing investments like bonds or dividend-paying stocks. Conversely, if you have a longer time horizon, you might lean towards growth-oriented investments like stocks or real estate.

Deciding whether to move your retirement account from a work fund to a new investment fund when you retire is an important consideration. Some

RETIREMENT PLANNING MADE EASY

prefer to roll over their 401(k) into an IRA for greater control and more investment options, while others may choose to keep their funds within the employer's plan. Each decision should be evaluated based on fees, investment choices, and how well they align with your evolving retirement strategy. This is a good time to sit down with a financial advisor so they can guide you through this transition and ensure you don't do anything to impact your tax position or your fund balance.

3.3 Adjusting Investments as You Age

As you near retirement, your investment strategy should evolve to reflect your changing financial landscape. The shift from growth-focused to income-focused investments becomes critical. During your working years, you might have prioritized high-growth stocks to build wealth. Now, as you enter retirement, stability and consistent income become paramount. This transition often involves increasing the proportion of bonds in your portfolio. Bonds provide regular interest payments, acting as a steady income stream. One effective strategy is bond laddering, where you stagger bond maturities over several years. This approach ensures a portion of your bonds mature annually, providing regular income while protecting against interest rate fluctuations. As your investment focus shifts, these adjustments help secure a stable financial base, ensuring your retirement funds last as long as you need them.

Life-cycle investment strategies offer an automated approach to adjusting your portfolio as you age. Target-date funds, for instance, automatically shift from growth-oriented investments to more conservative ones as the target retirement date approaches. They offer simplicity, requiring little hands-on management. However, some investors prefer customizing their strategies, tailoring asset allocation to personal needs and risk tolerance. Custom life-cycle strategies might involve manually adjusting your portfolio, allowing for greater flexibility and control. Whether you choose a target-date fund or a personalized approach, both strategies aim to balance risk and reward while adapting to your evolving financial goals. The key is finding a path that aligns with your comfort level and long-term objectives, ensuring your portfolio continues to support your lifestyle as you age.

Monitoring changes in your financial needs is essential as you transition into retirement. Regularly assessing your situation allows you to make informed decisions, aligning investments with your current goals. Life events such as a health change or unexpected expenses might necessitate adjustments to your strategy. You might need to increase liquidity or adjust your asset allocation to accommodate these changes. Engaging a financial advisor can offer valuable insights, helping you navigate complex decisions with confidence. Advisors provide personalized guidance, assessing your portfolio's performance and suggesting adjustments to optimize returns while managing risk. Their expertise can be particularly beneficial during periods of uncertainty, ensuring your investments remain aligned with your financial goals and evolving needs.

As you reach a certain age, typically 72, required minimum distributions (RMDs) from retirement accounts become a legal necessity. Understanding RMDs is crucial, as failing to withdraw the minimum amount can result in substantial penalties. Calculating RMDs involves dividing your account balance by a life expectancy factor, determined by IRS tables. Strategic timing of these withdrawals can minimize tax impact. For instance, consider spreading distributions throughout the year to avoid pushing yourself into a higher tax bracket. Another strategy involves withdrawing more than the minimum during years with lower income, allowing you to manage your tax liability effectively. Additionally, some retirees choose to convert a portion of their traditional IRA to a Roth IRA before RMDs begin. This conversion can reduce future RMDs and provide tax-free withdrawals later. Being proactive about RMDs helps preserve your wealth, ensuring your retirement funds are used efficiently and effectively throughout your lifetime.

3.4 Avoiding Common Investment Pitfalls

Investing is a path filled with opportunities, but it's also riddled with pitfalls that can derail even the most well-intentioned plans. One of the most common errors investors make is allowing emotions to dictate decisions, especially in volatile markets. When the stock market experiences significant swings, it's easy to fall into the trap of panic selling or impulsively buying, hoping to capitalize on short-term fluctuations. This emotional decision-making can lead to buying high and selling low, eroding your hard-earned savings. To avoid this, cultivate a disciplined approach, grounded in your long-term strategy, rather than reacting to daily market noise. Over-concentration in a single stock or sector is another pitfall. While it might seem enticing to invest heavily in a high-performing stock or an industry you believe in, this approach can backfire if that sector faces a downturn. Diversifying your investments across different industries and asset classes reduces risk and provides a buffer against unexpected market shifts.

Historical market trends offer invaluable lessons for today's investors. By studying past market bubbles and crashes, you can gain insights into the patterns and behaviors that often precede significant market events. The dot-com bubble of the late 1990s and the housing market crash of 2008 serve as stark reminders of the dangers of speculative excess and over-leveraging. These historical missteps underscore the importance of maintaining a balanced portfolio and avoiding the temptation of chasing after the latest market craze. Understanding that markets move in cycles helps temper expectations, allowing you to prepare for downturns and capitalize on upswings. This knowledge is a powerful tool, equipping you to sidestep common traps and make informed investment choices.

A disciplined investment approach is crucial for long-term success. This involves adhering to a well-defined strategy, often encapsulated in an investment policy statement (IPS). Your IPS acts as a personal blueprint, outlining your investment objectives, risk tolerance, and asset allocation guidelines. This is worth reviewing annually to ensure it's still relevant and updating it if necessary. It serves as a steadying force, guiding your decisions and helping you remain focused on your goals, even when markets are turbulent. Techniques for staying the course include setting realistic expectations, regularly reviewing your strategy, and resisting the urge to make impulsive changes based on short-term market movements. For those preferring a hands-off approach, investment houses and funds like Vanguard offer managed retirement accounts, where professionals oversee your portfolio, ensuring it aligns with your strategy and objectives. These services provide peace of mind, allowing you to enjoy retirement without the stress of daily investment management.

Continuous improvement in your investment strategy is achieved through incorporating feedback loops. Regularly reviewing and reflecting on your portfolio's performance enables you to identify areas for enhancement or adjustment. This process of self-assessment, when paired with feedback from financial advisors, allows for informed adaptations that refine your approach. Advisors can offer valuable insights, drawing on their expertise to highlight potential improvements or adjustments warranted by changing market conditions or personal circumstances. An example of a rebalanced portfolio from a company like Vanguard illustrates the benefits of this approach, showcasing how automatic adjustments can maintain your desired asset allocation without constant manual intervention. This ongoing process of learning and adaptation ensures that your investment strategy evolves with you, remaining effective and aligned with your retirement goals.

As you navigate the world of investments, remember that avoiding common pitfalls requires a blend of historical knowledge, disciplined strategies, and a commitment to continuous improvement. This proactive approach not only safeguards your financial future but also empowers you to make confident, informed decisions. As we transition into the next chapter, we'll explore how to integrate these investment choices into a comprehensive retirement plan, ensuring a future that's financially secure and fulfilling.

Don't move on to the next chapter without doing the following;

1. Log on to your retirement account online and understand what sort of fund you're enrolled in. Check it's performance for the last 3 years and it's expense ratio
2. Do you need to change your investment fund to something more or less aggressive depending on your life stage?
3. Go to Vanguard and fill out the risk questionnaire
4. Do you need to book a time with a financial advisor to begin transition out of work planning?

Chapter 4

Navigating Social Security

Picture this: you're entering your retirement years, ready to embrace the freedom that comes with it, yet there's a crucial piece of the puzzle called Social Security. It's a system that many rely on, yet few truly understand. Social Security benefits are like a dependable friend, one that has been around for decades, offering support when you need it most. But like any good relationship, understanding the details makes all the difference. This chapter aims to demystify Social Security, providing clarity on how benefits are calculated, who qualifies, and what types of benefits are available. It's about empowering you with knowledge, ensuring you're not only prepared but confident in making the best choices for your financial future.

4.1 Understanding Social Security

Understanding how Social Security benefits are calculated is the first step in unlocking it's potential. The calculation process is anchored in your work history and lifetime earnings, specifically focusing on your 35 highest-earning years. This period forms the backbone of your Average Indexed Monthly Earnings (AIME), a crucial figure in determining your benefits. The

Social Security Administration takes your earnings, adjusts them for inflation, and calculates this average to reflect your lifetime earnings capacity. Once your AIME is determined, the next step involves calculating your Primary Insurance Amount (PIA), which is the monthly benefit amount you receive at full retirement age. The PIA is calculated using a formula that applies bend points to your AIME: you receive 90% of the first $1,226, 32% of the AIME between $1,226 and $7,391, and 15% of any AIME above that threshold. This formula ensures that benefits are progressive, offering higher replacement rates for lower-income earners. Understanding these components not only clarifies how your benefits are determined but also highlights the importance of maximizing your earning years.

Eligibility for Social Security benefits is not automatic; it requires meeting specific criteria, primarily centered around work credits and age. To qualify for retirement benefits, you need to earn a minimum of 40 work credits, which equates to approximately 10 years of work. Each year, you can earn up to four credits, with one credit earned per $1,730 in wages or self-employment income (as of 2024). These credits are the building blocks of your eligibility, ensuring you've contributed enough to the system to receive benefits. Age is another factor, with full benefits available only when you reach your designated full retirement age, which ranges from 65 to 67 depending on your birth year. This threshold is critical, as claiming benefits before reaching full retirement age results in reduced monthly payments, while delaying can increase them. Understanding these eligibility requirements is essential, ensuring you meet the criteria needed to access your rightful benefits.

Social Security offers various types of benefits beyond traditional retirement income, each designed to support different life circumstances. Retirement benefits are the most common, providing a monthly income to retirees who have reached the appropriate age and credit requirements. Disability benefits, however, offer support to those who are unable to work due to a qualifying disability, ensuring financial stability in the face of health challenges. Survivor benefits provide crucial support to spouses and children in the event of a worker's death, allowing them to claim a portion of the deceased's benefits. These benefits ensure that Social Security serves as a multifaceted safety net, offering assistance tailored to a range of needs. Understanding the distinctions between retirement, disability, and survivor benefits is vital, allowing you to navigate the system effectively and maximize the support available to you and your family.

Misunderstandings about Social Security abound, often leading to misconceptions that can hinder effective planning. One prevalent myth is that Social Security should serve as the primary source of retirement income. While it's a valuable component, it's not designed to cover all expenses, typically replacing only a portion of pre-retirement income. This highlights the importance of having a diversified retirement income strategy, incorporating savings, investments, and other sources. Another common concern involves the sustainability of the Social Security fund. Worries about depletion often prompt questions about whether benefits will be available in the future. It's true that demographic shifts and funding challenges exist, but adjustments, such as changes to the wage base or benefit calculations, have historically maintained the program's solvency. By addressing these myths and providing accurate information, you can navigate Social Security with confidence, ensuring it complements your broader financial plans.

Reflection Section: Evaluating Your Social Security Knowledge

Consider what you've learned about Social Security, and reflect on the following questions:

- How does understanding your AIME and PIA influence your retirement planning?
- Are you on track to earn the necessary work credits for eligibility?
- Which type of Social Security benefits might you or your family qualify for in the future?
- How do these benefits fit into your overall retirement income strategy?
- What steps can you take to address any misconceptions or concerns about Social Security?

Reflecting on these questions will strengthen your understanding, helping you make informed decisions as you prepare for the future.

4.2 Timing Your Social Security Claims

The decision of when to claim Social Security benefits is more than just picking a date on the calendar; it's a strategic financial move that can significantly affect your monthly income. The age at which you decide to start receiving benefits plays a crucial role in determining the amount you'll collect each month. Claiming benefits at your full retirement age (FRA) will yield the full amount calculated based on your earnings record. However, if you choose to receive benefits before reaching your FRA, your monthly benefit is reduced, potentially by up to 30%, depending on how early you start. On the other hand, delaying your claim beyond your FRA can increase your benefits by approximately 8% for each year you postpone, up until age 70. This increase is due to delayed retirement credits, which can significantly enhance your financial security in later years. Understanding these options allows you to weigh the pros and cons, ensuring your decision aligns with your retirement goals and financial needs.

Understanding your full retirement age is a fundamental aspect of planning. Your FRA is determined by your birth year, with those born between 1943 and 1954 reaching FRA at 66, while those born in 1960 and later have an FRA of 67. This age is pivotal because it affects not only the size of your monthly benefit but also your eligibility for certain programs and credits. Knowing your FRA helps in strategizing the optimal time to claim benefits. If you decide to claim before reaching FRA, you'll face a reduction in benefits, while waiting can lead to increased payments. This knowledge empowers you to make informed decisions that suit your financial situation, family circumstances, and retirement timeline. By understanding these calculations, you gain clarity on how your choices today impact your financial well-being tomorrow.

Exploring the scenarios of early and delayed claims reveals a complex landscape of advantages and disadvantages. For some, claiming early at age 62 may seem appealing, providing immediate income and flexibility. However, this choice results in permanently reduced benefits and may not be ideal if you have a longer life expectancy. Delaying claims, conversely, offers increased monthly payments, enhancing your financial stability in the later stages of retirement. Consider the case of Susan, who decided to delay her benefits until age 70. This decision resulted in significantly higher monthly payments, providing her with greater financial freedom and peace of mind. Conversely, her friend Tom opted for early benefits due to immediate financial needs, accepting the trade-off of reduced income. Both scenarios underline the importance of evaluating personal circumstances, health, and financial needs when deciding on the timing of your benefits.

To further personalize your decision-making process, consider engaging in an exercise using online calculators to crunch your numbers e.g. Boldin. These tools allow you to input your specific details, such as current earnings, expected retirement age, and Social Secruity, providing a tailored estimate of your potential benefits. By modeling different scenarios, you can visualize the impact of various claiming strategies and make an informed choice that supports your retirement goals. This hands-on approach equips you with the knowledge and confidence needed to navigate the complexities of Social Security, ensuring your decisions are grounded in a comprehensive understanding of your unique situation.

Personal factors play a significant role in determining the best time to claim Social Security benefits. Health considerations are paramount; if you anticipate a shorter lifespan due to health issues, claiming earlier might make sense. Conversely, if longevity runs in your family, delaying benefits could maximize your lifetime income. Longevity projections, based on family history and personal health, offer valuable insights into how long you might expect to draw benefits. Additionally, consider your financial needs and other income sources. If you have sufficient retirement savings or alternative income streams, delaying Social Security could enhance your financial position in later years. Each factor intertwines, shaping your overall strategy and ensuring your choices reflect your personal circumstances and aspirations.

Navigating these decisions requires a balance of knowledge, foresight, and personal reflection. By understanding the mechanics of Social Security and evaluating your unique situation, you can craft a strategy that not only meets your immediate needs but also secures your financial future.

4.3 Strategies to Maximize Benefits

Navigating the intricacies of Social Security doesn't end at understanding your own benefits; it extends to maximizing the potential income for your family through spousal and survivor benefits. These Social Security features can significantly enhance your household's financial well-being if used strategically. For spouses, Social Security offers benefits up to 50% of the working partner's full retirement amount. This is particularly beneficial when one spouse has a significantly lower lifetime earnings record. For example, if your primary benefit is more substantial, your spouse can opt for spousal benefits, potentially increasing your combined income. However, it's crucial to coordinate these benefits carefully to ensure you're maximizing your family's Social Security income. Survivor benefits further provide financial security, allowing a surviving spouse or dependent children to receive benefits based on the deceased's earnings record. This support can be a lifeline, ensuring that financial stability continues even after the loss of a loved one. Understanding how and when to claim these benefits is key to optimizing your family's financial strategy under Social Security.

For those who choose—or need—to continue working while receiving Social Security benefits, understanding how earnings affect your benefits is vital. If you haven't yet reached your full retirement age and decide to work while collecting Social Security, your earnings can impact the benefits you receive. There are set earnings limits for those below full retirement age; for every $2 earned over the limit, $1 is withheld from your benefits. Once you reach your full retirement age, this earnings cap is lifted, allowing you to earn without reductions to your Social Security income. However, any benefits withheld while you were under the earnings limit aren't lost; they're recalculated and credited back to you once you reach full retirement age, potentially increasing your monthly benefit. This recalibration can sometimes offset the initial reduction, providing a boost to your long-term financial outlook while allowing you to enjoy the benefits of continued employment. There are online calculators on the www.ssa.gov website or give them a call to ask the question.

Maximizing your Social Security benefits also involves understanding their tax implications and employing strategies to minimize tax liabilities during retirement. Social Security benefits can be taxable, depending on your combined income. This includes your adjusted gross income, nontaxable interest, and half of your Social Security benefits. If your combined income exceeds certain thresholds, up to 85% of your benefits may be taxable. To manage this, consider strategies that minimize your taxable income. One approach is to strategically withdraw from retirement accounts, balancing your income to stay within lower tax brackets. Additionally, converting traditional IRAs to Roth IRAs before reaching retirement age can help, as Roth withdrawals are tax-free and don't count towards your taxable income. These methods not only reduce your immediate tax burden but also preserve more of your benefits for future use. Tax is an ever evolving subject and requires advice from a financial advisor. It might be worth booking in an appointment before these transition years to help understand and optimize your tax planning.

Inflation is another factor that can impact the real value of your Social Security benefits over time. Social Security benefits are adjusted for inflation through cost-of-living adjustments (COLAs), designed to maintain purchasing power as prices rise. Historically, these adjustments have varied, reflecting changes in the economic environment. While COLAs provide some protection against inflation, they may not fully match the actual rise in living costs, especially for healthcare and other essentials. Planning for inflation-adjusted income needs is crucial, ensuring that your benefits maintain their value over the years. This might involve supplementing your Social Security with other income sources or investments that offer growth potential to counteract inflation's effects. Understanding these dynamics allows you to make informed decisions, ensuring your retirement income remains robust despite economic fluctuations.

4.4 Coordinating Social Security with Other Income Sources

Integrating Social Security into your overall retirement income plan is akin to piecing together a financial puzzle, where each component plays a crucial role in ensuring a stable and secure future. Social Security often serves as the foundation, offering a predictable stream of income that can be relied upon throughout retirement. However, to build a robust plan, it's essential to weave this income source with other elements like pensions, savings, and investments. Creating a comprehensive retirement income plan involves assessing all potential income streams, understanding their interplay, and strategizing for maximum efficiency and sustainability. This holistic approach not only enhances financial security but also provides the flexibility needed to adapt to life's unexpected changes. By considering Social Security as a foundational element and coordinating it with other income sources, you position yourself to enjoy a retirement that is both secure and fulfilling.

Balancing Social Security with pension and investment income requires careful planning to avoid pitfalls and maximize benefits. Pensions, often a significant part of retirement income, provide a regular payment based on your employment history. Coordinating these payments with Social Security requires an understanding of how they fit together, avoiding any overlap that might lead to penalties. For instance, some pensions, especially those from government jobs, may affect your Social Security benefits through mechanisms like the Windfall Elimination Provision. Strategic withdrawals from retirement accounts, such as IRAs and 401(k)s, also play a vital role in this balance. Timing these withdrawals to align with your Social Security benefits can minimize tax consequences and ensure a steady income stream.

Understanding the tax implications of different income sources is crucial, as excessive withdrawals can push you into a higher tax bracket, reducing your net income. This careful orchestration ensures that all components work harmoniously, providing the financial support you need without unnecessary burdens.

Required Minimum Distributions (RMDs) from retirement accounts add another layer of complexity to your Social Security planning. RMDs are mandatory withdrawals that begin at age 73 (as of the SECURE 2.0 Act), designed to ensure that tax-deferred retirement savings are eventually taxed. The timing of RMDs can affect your Social Security benefits, especially if the withdrawals increase your taxable income significantly. Coordinating RMDs with Social Security requires a strategic approach, considering both tax efficiency and income needs. For example, spreading RMDs throughout the year rather than taking them all at once can prevent a spike in taxable income, preserving more of your Social Security benefits. Another strategy might involve withdrawing more than the required minimum during years with lower income, thereby managing your tax liability effectively. By planning RMDs carefully, you maintain control over your financial landscape, ensuring that both Social Security and retirement savings work in concert to support your lifestyle.

In an ever-changing economic environment, preparing for potential benefit reductions is a realistic and prudent step in retirement planning. While Social Security provides a reliable income stream, future changes could impact benefit levels due to demographic shifts or policy adjustments. Contingency planning for such reductions involves diversifying your income streams, ensuring that you are not overly reliant on any single source. This diversification might include exploring part-time work, investing in income-generating assets, or even considering annuities that offer guaranteed payouts. By spreading risk across multiple sources, you build resilience into your financial plan, mitigating the impact of any one change. Additionally, regularly reviewing your retirement plan allows you to adapt to new circumstances, ensuring that your strategy remains aligned with your goals and the broader economic landscape.

Exercise: Include Social Security in Your Retirement Cashflow

To see the full picture of your retirement finances, it's crucial to integrate Social Security into your cash flow planning. In Chapter 1 we listed income and expenses in the template. Now you can update the In Retirement column. Start by listing all potential income sources, including pensions, investments, and any part-time work. Calculate your expected Social Security benefits using your estimated claiming age. This is available online at www.ssa.gov and check out their online calculators. Next, outline your anticipated expenses, both fixed and variable. Compare this total to your projected income, identifying any gaps that need addressing that could be filled from your retirement account. This exercise not only highlights the role of Social Security in your overall plan but also provides a clear view of your financial needs, allowing you to make informed decisions about savings, investments, and lifestyle choices. By understanding your cash flow, you can adjust your strategy to ensure a balanced and sustainable retirement.

In summary, integrating Social Security with other income sources requires strategic coordination, careful consideration of tax implications, and a proactive approach to potential changes. By understanding the interplay between different income streams and planning accordingly, you create a retirement strategy that supports your lifestyle and financial goals. This chapter provides the tools and insights needed to navigate these complexities, ensuring that you are well-prepared for the road ahead. As you move forward, consider how these strategies can be applied to your unique situation, empowering you to make confident and informed decisions about your retirement future.

Don't move on to the next chapter without doing the following;

1. Have you logged in to www.ssa.gov to determine your eligibility for Social Security and what benefits you would receive at different ages? If not do that now
2. Log in to Boldin and look at the different scenarios around what age

you claim Social Security and when will you stop work. It will show you graphically the differences in your portfolio balance if you do these changes

3. Do you need to book in a meeting with a financial advisor to understand the different tax scenarios?

4. Update the Social Security income into your Income and Expenses template in Chapter 1. Update this in Boldin too

Chapter 5

Healthcare and Long-Term Care Planning

Picture this: you're ready to enjoy your golden years, basking in the freedom that retirement promises. Yet, lurking behind this idyllic vision is the potential financial burden of healthcare costs. It's a reality that many overlook, but it's as essential to your retirement planning as saving and investing. Healthcare expenses can be a significant concern, particularly as you age and potentially face more medical needs. Understanding and preparing for these costs ensures you can enjoy your retirement without the stress of unexpected medical bills.

The trajectory of healthcare costs over the years serves as a cautionary tale. In 1970, U.S. health spending was a modest $74.1 billion. Fast forward to 2022, and that figure has skyrocketed to $4.5 trillion. That's an increase driven by various factors such as technological advancements, aging populations, and rising prices for services and drugs. According to recent data, health spending has been growing consistently, with hospital expenditures and retail prescription drugs being significant contributors. From 2021 to 2022 alone, national health expenditures grew by $175 billion. This rapid escalation emphasizes the need for a proactive approach to healthcare planning in retirement.

Understanding where these costs typically arise can help you better prepare. Routine medical care and check-ups are foundational to maintaining health, accounting for regular visits to your primary care physician and necessary screenings. Prescription medications and therapies are another substantial category, often critical in managing chronic conditions or supporting recovery. The cost of hospitalization and emergency services can be significant, especially if unexpected health issues arise. Hospitals accounted for 30.4% of total health spending in 2022, and with the prices of medical services steadily increasing, preparing for such expenses is crucial.

Projecting your future healthcare needs involves more than just guessing based on age. It requires a thoughtful assessment of your current health status and family medical history. Health risk assessment tools are invaluable in this process and there are many online calculators. Try https://familyhealthriskca lculator.osumc.edu/. They evaluate your lifestyle, medical history, and family background to predict potential health issues. For example, a family history of heart disease might suggest a need for regular cardiovascular screenings. Analyzing potential future scenarios allows you to anticipate the types of care you may require and plan accordingly. Case studies often reveal that projected healthcare costs can vary widely from actual expenses, underscoring the importance of a personalized assessment. A proactive approach can help anticipate these needs, ensuring you're financially prepared for whatever health challenges may come your way.

Incorporating healthcare costs into your retirement planning is not just wise; it's necessary. Start by modifying your retirement budget (that we did in Chapter 1&4) that explicitly includes healthcare expenses. This budget should reflect both current costs and anticipated increases, as healthcare inflation outpaces general inflation. For instance, a typical 65-year-old may need approximately $165,000 in after-tax income for healthcare expenses in retirement. Incorporating such significant figures into your budget ensures you're not caught off guard. Techniques for adjusting retirement savings to cover these costs include setting aside a dedicated healthcare fund or increasing contributions to existing retirement accounts during your working years. These adjustments help create a financial buffer, providing peace of mind and financial security.

Reflection Section: Estimating Your Healthcare Costs

Take a moment to reflect on your current health and future needs. Consider the following:

- What routine healthcare services do you currently use, and how might they change in retirement? e.g. primary physician, cardiologist for heart checks or annual colonoscopy
- Do you have a family history of medical conditions that could affect your future healthcare needs?
- How will you incorporate projected healthcare costs into your retirement budget?
- Are there areas where you can increase your savings to address potential healthcare expenses? Or will your retirement account cover the projected expense?

Reflecting on these questions will help you create a comprehensive plan, ensuring that your healthcare needs are met without compromising your financial security in retirement.

5.1 Medicare: What You Need to Know

Navigating the world of Medicare can often feel overwhelming, especially as you approach the age when these decisions become critical. Medicare is a federal health insurance program primarily for individuals aged 65 and older, though it also covers certain younger people with disabilities. Eligibility typically requires that you or your spouse have worked and paid into the Medicare system through payroll taxes. Understanding the enrollment process is crucial to avoid penalties. There are specific periods when you can enroll: the Initial Enrollment Period, which spans seven months around your 65th birthday; the General Enrollment Period from January 1 to March 31 each year; and Special Enrollment Periods triggered by specific life events. Missing these windows can result in higher premiums, underscoring the importance of timely enrollment.

Medicare is composed of several parts, each covering different aspects of healthcare. Part A, often called hospital insurance, covers inpatient hospital stays, care in a skilled nursing facility, hospice care, and some home health care. It's typically premium-free if you or your spouse paid Medicare taxes for a certain amount of time. Part B involves medical insurance, covering specific doctors services, outpatient care, medical supplies, and preventive services. Part B requires a monthly premium, which varies based on income. Part C, or Medicare Advantage, offers an alternative way to receive your Medicare benefits through private insurance companies that contract with Medicare. These plans often include additional benefits such as vision, hearing, and dental coverage. Lastly, Part D provides prescription drug coverage, helping cover the cost of medications. Understanding these parts allows you to make informed decisions tailored to your health needs and financial circumstances.

Choosing the right Medicare plan involves evaluating your current and anticipated healthcare needs. Original Medicare, which includes Parts A and B, offers flexibility in choosing healthcare providers but leaves gaps in coverage, such as for prescription drugs, long-term care, and routine dental or vision care. Many opt for supplemental insurance, like Medigap policies, to cover these gaps. Medigap plans are standardized and sold by private companies, helping pay some out-of-pocket costs not covered by Original Medicare. On the other hand, Medicare Advantage plans can provide a convenient all-in-one alternative. These plans often include Part D coverage and additional benefits but may require you to use a network of doctors and hospitals. Deciding between Original Medicare and Medicare Advantage depends on factors such as your preferred healthcare providers, travel habits, and whether you need additional coverage for services not included in Original Medicare.

Understanding the costs associated with Medicare is pivotal for effective budgeting. Part A usually doesn't require a monthly premium if you've paid Medicare taxes for at least ten years, but it does come with a deductible and possible coinsurance. Part B requires a monthly premium—$174.70 in 2024—and an annual deductible. Once the deductible is met, you typically pay 20% of the Medicare-approved amount for most doctor services. Part D premiums vary by plan and income, with an average basic premium of $55.50 in 2024. Out-of-pocket costs can quickly add up, especially if you require frequent medical attention or expensive prescriptions. Strategies to manage these expenses include selecting plans with lower premiums if you're in good health or opting for more comprehensive coverage if you anticipate higher medical needs. Additionally, some might find value in Medicare Savings Programs, which can help pay for some of the costs associated with Medicare.

A common misconception is that Medicare will cover all your healthcare expenses, which is far from the truth. While it provides essential coverage, it doesn't include everything. Services like long-term care, dental care, vision care, and hearing aids often fall outside its scope. This gap can lead to unexpected expenses if you're unprepared. Addressing these shortcomings might involve investing in supplemental insurance or saving specifically for uncovered expenses. Moreover, understanding what Medicare does and doesn't cover can prevent costly surprises. For instance, while Medicare provides some short-term care in nursing facilities, it doesn't cover long-term care, which many may require as they age. Being aware of these limitations ensures you can plan effectively, integrating these considerations into your broader financial strategy.

Exercise: Integrating Medicare into Your Cash Flow Planning

Consider how Medicare fits into your overall retirement budget. Reflect on the following:

- Have you identified which parts of Medicare you need, based on your health and financial situation?
- Are you aware of the out-of-pocket costs associated with your chosen Medicare plan?
- Have you factored potential gaps not covered by Medicare into your budget?
- What steps can you take to manage unexpected healthcare costs not covered by Medicare?

If you have any questions about what is and isn't covered call Medicare on 1-800-MEDICARE to get your questions answered. These reflections will help you incorporate Medicare effectively into your retirement planning, ensuring a comprehensive approach to managing healthcare costs.

5.2 Exploring Long-Term Care Insurance Options

As you look toward retirement, planning for long-term care should be a priority. Long-term care encompasses a variety of services designed to meet health or personal care needs over an extended period. Unlike acute care, which is short-term and focused on recovery, long-term care helps individuals manage chronic illnesses, disabilities, or other conditions that limit their ability to perform everyday activities. Services can range from home health care—where professionals assist with daily tasks like bathing and dressing— to more intensive care in facilities such as nursing homes or assisted living centers. It's a reality that more than half of Americans over 65 will require some form of long-term care during their lives. This statistic underscores the importance of considering how you'll manage these potential needs. Planning for long-term care is not only about securing your comfort but also protecting your financial resources, ensuring you won't deplete your savings or burden your family with unexpected costs.

Evaluating long-term care insurance policies involves understanding the various options available and how they fit into your financial plan. Long-term care insurance is designed to cover services not typically covered by health insurance, Medicare, or Medicaid. When comparing policies, consider the features and benefits each offers. Key aspects include the daily benefit amount, which determines how much the policy will pay for each day of care. Also, examine the benefit period, which is the length of time benefits are payable. Policy features might also include inflation protection, which adjusts your benefits to keep pace with rising costs. Another crucial component is the elimination period, which is the waiting time before benefits begin, which can range from 30 to 90 days. Choosing a longer elimination period might reduce your premium but requires you to pay for initial care out of pocket. Benefit triggers are conditions under which benefits are paid, usually tied to the inability to perform a certain number of activities of daily living or cognitive impairment. Understanding these terms helps you select a policy tailored to your needs, ensuring that you're adequately covered when the time comes.

Several factors influence the cost of long-term care insurance policies. Your age and health status at the time of purchase significantly affect premiums. Generally, the younger and healthier you are, the lower the premium. This is because insurers perceive a lower risk, given that you're less likely to need care in the near term. However, as you age or if health issues arise, premiums can increase, making it crucial to consider buying a policy sooner rather than later. Additionally, the duration of coverage you choose impacts cost. Longer benefit periods or higher daily benefits will naturally increase the premium. Inflation protection is another factor; policies with this feature tend to be more expensive but provide peace of mind as they help your benefits keep up with the rising cost of care. Balancing these factors against your budget and potential needs is essential for selecting the most suitable policy. These policies are also tax deductible in your tax return each year.

Beyond traditional long-term care insurance, there are alternative strategies to consider. Hybrid policies, which combine life insurance with long-term care coverage, are increasingly popular. These policies provide the flexibility of a death benefit if long-term care is not needed, or they can be drawn upon for care expenses. While they tend to be more costly upfront, the dual benefit can be appealing for those seeking a more versatile option. Another alternative is utilizing Health Savings Accounts (HSAs) for long-term care expenses. HSAs offer tax advantages, allowing you to pay for qualified medical expenses, including long-term care, with pre-tax dollars. This approach is particularly beneficial if you already have an HSA from your working years, as it can be a tax-efficient way to handle future healthcare costs. These alternatives offer different pathways to manage long-term care needs, providing flexibility and options beyond traditional insurance. Never fear if you don't have long term care insurance as you can pay for care out of pocket but it will likely be more expensive than if you did it via long term care insurance.

As you explore these options, it's important to integrate them into your overall financial plan. Reflect on your current situation and consider how long-term care might fit into your retirement strategy. Consider an exercise to factor this into your cash flow planning from Chapter 1. Assess your existing resources, the potential need for long-term care, and how you might accommodate these costs within your budget. This proactive approach ensures that you're not only prepared for the expected but also resilient in the face of unforeseen challenges.

5.3 Planning for Unexpected Medical Expenses

In the landscape of retirement, unexpected medical expenses can emerge as formidable challenges, threatening the financial stability you've worked so hard to maintain. Such unforeseen costs often arise from emergency surgeries or hospitalizations, where the urgency of care leaves little room for financial maneuvering. Imagine a sudden need for a joint replacement or an unexpected heart procedure. These situations can lead to substantial bills, especially if you find yourself needing specialized care outside of your insurance network. Out-of-network specialist consultations, while sometimes necessary for optimal health outcomes, can also contribute to unexpectedly high expenses. Such consultations might be required when dealing with a rare condition or seeking a second opinion from a renowned expert. Navigating these costs without preparation can quickly strain your retirement budget, making it crucial to anticipate and plan for such scenarios.

Creating a dedicated emergency healthcare fund is a proactive strategy to buffer against these unforeseen expenses. This fund acts as a financial safety net, providing the reassurance that you can access necessary care without compromising your financial security. Setting targets for this fund involves considering your individual health needs and potential risks. A good rule of thumb is to aim for at least six months worth of expenses, though your specific target might vary based on personal circumstances and risk factors. Funding and maintaining this reserve can be approached incrementally. Consider setting aside a portion of your monthly income or reallocating funds from other savings. Regularly contributing to this fund, even in small amounts, builds a cushion over time. This disciplined approach ensures that when medical surprises occur, you have the resources to manage them without derailing your financial plans.

Supplemental insurance options play a significant role in covering gaps that traditional health insurance might leave. Medigap policies, for instance, are designed to fill the voids left by Medicare, covering costs like co-payments, coinsurance, and deductibles. These policies can be tailored to your specific needs, ensuring you're not left vulnerable to high out-of-pocket expenses. Critical illness insurance offers another layer of protection, providing a lump-sum payment if you're diagnosed with a severe illness such as cancer or heart disease. This payout can be used for a variety of needs, including treatment costs, recovery expenses, or even everyday living expenses while you focus on your health. Understanding these options allows you to choose the coverage that aligns with your potential risks, ensuring comprehensive protection against the financial impact of severe medical events.

Adopting proactive health management strategies can also mitigate the risk of unexpected medical issues. Regular health screenings and wellness check-ups are integral components of preventive care, catching potential issues before they escalate into costly emergencies. These screenings might include routine blood tests, cancer screenings, or cardiovascular assessments, all tailored to your age and health history. Additionally, embracing a healthy lifestyle through balanced nutrition and regular exercise can significantly reduce the likelihood of developing chronic conditions. Simple changes, like incorporating more fruits and vegetables into your diet or taking daily walks, can have a profound impact on your overall well-being. These proactive measures not only contribute to better health outcomes but also reduce the chances of incurring unexpected medical costs.

Exercise: Planning for the Unexpected

Reflect on your current health management practices and consider how you might enhance them. Ask yourself:

- What potential emergency medical situations could you face based on your health history?
- Have you established an emergency healthcare fund, and how can you grow it?
- Are there supplemental insurance options that could fill gaps in your current coverage?
- How can you integrate regular health screenings and lifestyle changes into your routine?

By contemplating these questions, you can develop a more robust strategy to protect your financial health alongside your physical health.

As we've navigated through the intricacies of healthcare and long-term care planning, it's clear that preparation is key to safeguarding your retirement. These strategies not only protect your financial well-being but also ensure peace of mind. There is a lot of meat in this chapter and a lot of potential costs you'll need to anticipate. Methodically write them all down and research them then cost each option. As we move forward, consider how these elements integrate with your broader financial plan, preparing you for a retirement that's both secure and fulfilling.

Don't move on to the next chapter without doing the following;

1. Have you filled in an online health risk assessment calculator?
2. Put in your diary or phone the initial enrollment date for Medicare so you don't miss enrolling around your 65th birthday
3. Do your research on Medicare A-D and what you will be covered for and how much it will cost. Good website for information is National Council on Aging or ring Medicare direct on 1-800-MEDICARE

4. Speak to a long term care insurance agent to understand the premiums now, when you retire or if you didn't have insurance at all and incorporate that into your Income and Expenses budget
5. Investigate what supplemental insurance covers and how much it costs
6. Create an account to build your emergency healthcare fund. Decide how you will invest this money

Chapter 6

Estate and Legacy Planning

Imagine a treasure map, where the 'X' marks the spot of your life's hard-earned wealth and cherished belongings. Now, picture leaving behind a clear path for your loved ones to follow, ensuring they receive what you intended when you are no longer there to guide them. Estate planning is this map, a crucial guide to ensure that your assets are distributed according to your wishes. Without it, your family might face unnecessary legal battles, stress, and even financial loss. This chapter delves into the essentials of wills and trusts, empowering you to create a legacy plan that reflects your values and intentions.

6.1 Basics of Wills and Trusts

A will is a legal document that outlines how you want your assets distributed after your death. It serves as a foundation for your estate plan, providing clarity and direction for your loved ones. Key elements of a will include the appointment of an executor, designation of beneficiaries, and a detailed list of assets. The executor is responsible for carrying out the terms of your will, ensuring everything is settled as you intended. Beneficiaries are the individuals or entities you wish to inherit your assets, which can range from family members to charities. Legal requirements for a valid will vary by state but generally include being of sound mind, having a written document, and signing it in the presence of witnesses. Without a will, your estate enters intestacy, where state laws dictate asset distribution, potentially leading to conflicts and unintended outcomes. The absence of a will isn't just legally troublesome; it can cause significant emotional distress for your family, leaving them to navigate complex probate processes without your guidance. Failing to create a will is fiscally irresponsible, as it may lead to higher estate taxes and legal costs, diminishing the value of what you leave behind.

Trusts offer an alternative or complementary approach to wills, allowing for more control over asset distribution. Unlike wills, which take effect after death, trusts can manage assets during your lifetime. Revocable trusts, also known as living trusts, provide flexibility, allowing you to modify terms or dissolve the trust as your circumstances change. They are particularly useful for managing assets if you become incapacitated, as they grant a trustee authority to manage your affairs. Irrevocable trusts, once established, cannot be altered without beneficiary consent, offering benefits such as asset protection from creditors and potential tax advantages. Special needs trusts are designed for beneficiaries with disabilities, ensuring they receive support without affecting their eligibility for government benefits. Trusts can serve various purposes beyond these, such as controlling beneficiaries' spending through spendthrift trusts or supporting charitable causes with charitable trusts. Each trust type addresses specific needs, providing tailored solutions to your estate planning challenges.

The benefits of trusts extend beyond asset management. One significant advantage is avoiding probate, the often lengthy and costly court process required to validate a will and distribute assets. By sidestepping probate, trusts enable a more private and efficient transfer of wealth, sparing your beneficiaries unnecessary delay and expense. Trusts also offer tax benefits, as strategic planning can reduce estate taxes, preserving more of your legacy for those you care about. Additionally, trusts protect assets from creditors, safeguarding your family's financial future. This protection is particularly valuable if you're concerned about potential legal claims or financial mismanagement by beneficiaries. By providing control over asset distribution, trusts allow you to specify the terms and conditions under which your assets are accessed, ensuring they are used in ways that reflect your values and intentions. This level of precision can offer peace of mind, knowing your legacy will be handled with care and respect.

Creating and maintaining wills and trusts requires thoughtful planning and professional guidance. Working with an estate planning attorney ensures your documents are legally sound and reflect your current wishes. An attorney can help you navigate the complexities of estate laws, tailoring your plan to your unique circumstances. Regular document reviews and updates are crucial, as life changes such as marriage, divorce, or the birth of a child can significantly impact your estate plan. It's essential to revisit these documents periodically, ensuring they remain aligned with your intentions and legal requirements. Consider setting reminders for yourself to review your estate plan at least every three to five years or after any major life event. By keeping your documents current, you ensure your estate plan continues to serve your goals, providing security and clarity for your loved ones when they need it most.

Reflection Section: Crafting Your Estate Plan

As you consider your estate planning needs, reflect on these questions to guide your next steps:

- Have you created a will that clearly outlines your wishes and includes all necessary legal components?
- Are there trusts that could enhance your estate plan, providing benefits such as probate avoidance or tax advantages?
- Have you worked with an estate planning attorney to ensure your documents are legally sound?
- How often do you review and update your estate plan to reflect changes in your life or financial situation?

These reflections will help you navigate the complexities of estate planning, ensuring your legacy is preserved according to your wishes.

6.2 Choosing and Updating Beneficiaries

Imagine setting a beautifully laid table for a family dinner, only to forget to invite your guests. This analogy reflects the crucial role of beneficiaries in estate planning. Designating beneficiaries is not merely an administrative task; it's the heart of your estate plan. By naming specific individuals for your retirement accounts and insurance policies, you ensure that your assets transfer directly to your chosen heirs without unnecessary delays or legal hurdles. This direct transfer can often bypass the probate process, allowing for a smoother and faster distribution of your assets. However, neglecting to name beneficiaries, or leaving them unspecified, can lead to unintended consequences. Assets might end up in the general estate, subject to probate and state law distribution, which can be both time-consuming and costly. Without clear designations, the fate of your assets could be decided by courts, not by your wishes, leading to possible disputes and emotional strain among your loved ones.

Choosing the right beneficiaries requires thoughtful consideration. It's about more than just listing names; it's about understanding the financial needs and capabilities of those you choose. Consider their current financial situation, their ability to manage the assets responsibly, and any future needs they may have. Family dynamics also play a significant role. Relationships can be complex, and your choices should reflect a balance that considers personal relationships and family harmony. For instance, while you might want to provide for a child with special needs, you must also ensure that their inheritance doesn't jeopardize their access to government assistance. Naming a special needs trust as a beneficiary in such cases can provide the necessary support without affecting their benefits. By evaluating these factors, you create a plan that supports your loved ones in a way that aligns with your intentions.

Regularly updating your beneficiary designations is as crucial as choosing them initially. Life is full of changes—marriages, divorces, births, and deaths—each affecting your estate plan. These events should trigger a review of your designations to ensure they remain current. An outdated beneficiary designation can lead to assets being distributed to individuals you no longer wish to benefit or excluding new family members unintentionally. For example, failing to update your beneficiaries after a divorce might result in your ex-spouse receiving assets you intended for your children. Such oversights can create financial and emotional complications for your family. By making it a habit to review your designations after significant life changes, you maintain control over your asset distribution, ensuring that your estate plan reflects your current wishes and circumstances.

Clear and legally binding beneficiary designations require precision in language and coordination. Use specific language in your designation forms to eliminate ambiguity. Instead of vague terms like "my children," list full names and Social Security numbers to prevent confusion. When dealing with multiple accounts, ensure that your designations are consistent and complementary. This coordination prevents discrepancies that could lead to legal disputes or unintended distributions. Additionally, consider naming contingent beneficiaries—those who will inherit if the primary beneficiary predeceases you or cannot accept the inheritance. This foresight adds a layer of security, ensuring your assets are distributed according to your wishes, even if circumstances change unexpectedly. By implementing these strategies, you create a robust and adaptable estate plan that respects your intentions and protects your loved ones.

6.3 Communicating Your Estate Plans

Imagine the relief of knowing your loved ones understand and respect your wishes long after you're gone. Transparent communication is the cornerstone of effective estate planning, helping to prevent disputes that can otherwise arise from misunderstandings or assumptions. By openly discussing your plans with family members, you reduce the risk of conflict and confusion, offering clarity and certainty about asset distribution. Transparency builds trust, allowing your family to feel included and informed. When you communicate openly, you empower your loved ones to grasp not just the financial aspects of your estate, but the values and intentions behind your decisions. This understanding fosters an atmosphere of cooperation and respect, reinforcing family bonds even in challenging times.

Initiating conversations about estate planning with family members might feel daunting, but it is necessary. Choose the right moment, perhaps during a calm family gathering, when tensions are low and everyone is more likely to be receptive. Aim for a setting that encourages openness and comfort, such as a living room or around a dinner table. Approach sensitive topics with compassion and empathy, acknowledging the emotions they may evoke. It's important to listen actively, giving space for questions and concerns. Encourage dialogue by expressing your intentions clearly, avoiding jargon that might confuse or alienate. This approach not only clarifies your wishes but also reassures your family that their feelings are considered and respected.

A comprehensive estate plan summary can be an invaluable tool, serving as a concise document that outlines the key aspects of your estate plan. This summary should include essential elements such as the location of your will and trust documents, a list of assets and liabilities, and contact information for your executor and legal advisors. Sharing this summary with executors and beneficiaries ensures everyone has access to the information they need when the time comes. It acts as a guide, reducing the burden on your family to piece together your intentions during an already emotional time. By providing this document, you offer a tangible reference that reinforces your plans, minimizing the potential for misunderstandings or oversight.

Despite your best efforts, conflicts may still arise during estate planning discussions. Addressing these proactively can prevent them from escalating. Mediation offers a constructive approach, providing a neutral space where family members can express their concerns and work towards resolution. A skilled mediator can facilitate dialogue, helping parties find common ground and understand each other's perspectives. If disagreements persist, legal avenues may be necessary to resolve disputes. Consulting with an estate attorney can provide clarity on legal rights and responsibilities, guiding you through the process of reaching a fair and equitable solution. By anticipating conflicts and preparing strategies for resolution, you ensure that your estate plan remains intact and your wishes are honored.

Reflection Section: Encouraging Open Dialogue

Consider these questions to facilitate open communication with your family about your estate plans:

- Have you chosen a suitable time and place to discuss your estate plans with your loved ones?
- Are you prepared to address sensitive topics with empathy and clarity?
- Have you created a summary of your estate plan to share with executors and beneficiaries?
- What potential conflicts might arise, and how can you address them through the preparation or updating of your will now, rather than when you it's too late when you pass away?

Reflecting on these questions will help you navigate the complexities of estate planning communication, ensuring your legacy is protected and respected.

6.4 Navigating the Emotional Aspects of Legacy Planning

Estate planning is more than a list of assets to distribute; it's a deeply personal process that stirs a range of emotions. You might experience feelings of vulnerability or apprehension as you confront your mortality and the reality of leaving loved ones behind. There might be a sense of fulfillment in knowing you are providing for your family, but also anxiety about making the right decisions. These emotions are normal and acknowledging them is the first step toward managing the stress they can bring. Consider mindfulness practices or meditation to help maintain calm and clarity. Regularly remind yourself of the purpose behind your planning: to ensure peace and security for those you leave behind. It's essential to approach estate planning with a balanced mindset and to seek support when needed—whether from friends, family, or professional counselors who specialize in these sensitive discussions.

Leaving a legacy extends beyond the tangible assets in your estate. It's about imparting values, creating lasting memories, and making a difference in the lives of others. Consider charitable giving as a way to contribute to causes you care deeply about, whether it's supporting education, the environment, or medical research. Philanthropy can be a powerful tool to extend your impact beyond your immediate circle, weaving your values into the fabric of community and society. Another way to solidify your legacy is by crafting a family mission statement. This document encapsulates your core beliefs and guiding principles, serving as a moral compass for future generations. It encourages unity and purpose, providing a shared foundation for your descendants to build upon. By thinking about what you wish to leave behind, you imbue your estate plan with deeper meaning and intentionality.

Reflecting on personal values and goals is crucial to aligning your estate plan with what truly matters to you. Start by identifying your core values through introspection or discussions with those closest to you. Ask yourself what legacy you want to leave and what principles you hope your family will carry forward. Exercises like journaling or creating a vision board can help clarify these priorities, offering a visual representation of your aspirations. An example of value-driven legacy planning might involve setting up a scholarship fund in your name, supporting young people in pursuing their dreams just as you once did. Or, perhaps it's as simple as ensuring your family continues a cherished tradition that holds sentimental value. By grounding your estate plan in your values, you ensure that your legacy reflects the essence of who you are and what you stand for.

Navigating the emotional terrain of estate planning can be challenging, but you don't have to go it alone. There are resources available to help you cope with these complexities. Counseling and support groups offer a safe space to express your concerns and receive guidance from professionals or peers who understand your situation. Literature and workshops focused on legacy planning can provide additional insights, offering strategies and perspectives that might resonate with your experience. These resources can be invaluable not only in managing the emotional aspects of estate planning but also in enriching your understanding of how to craft a legacy that aligns with your deepest values. Reaching out for support can transform what may seem like an overwhelming task into a process of empowerment and clarity, ensuring that you leave behind a legacy you and your loved ones can take pride in.

6.5 Avoiding Common Estate Planning Mistakes

Embarking on estate planning without a compass can lead to unnecessary pitfalls. One frequent mistake is neglecting to update documents regularly. Life is dynamic—families grow, relationships change, and financial situations evolve. Yet many people file away their wills and trusts, thinking the job is done. This oversight can result in outdated documents that no longer reflect your current wishes or family structure. Imagine the complications if a loved one is unintentionally excluded from a will, or worse, if an estranged relative remains a beneficiary. Regular updates ensure that your estate plan stays relevant, honoring your true intentions and minimizing potential conflicts. Overlooking digital assets is another misstep in the modern era. Today's estate extends beyond physical possessions to include online accounts, digital currencies, and even social media profiles. Without clear instructions, these assets can become inaccessible, leading to loss of value and personal memories. As part of your estate plan, consider listing these digital assets and providing access information, ensuring they are managed according to your wishes. Professional guidance is invaluable in navigating the complexities of estate planning. Consulting with an estate planning attorney or financial advisor can prevent costly mistakes that might arise from misunderstandings of the law or financial intricacies. These experts offer insights into the nuances of estate taxes, asset protection, and legal requirements, ensuring your plan is both effective and compliant. They can help you craft a strategy that aligns with your goals while navigating potential legal pitfalls. Comprehensive estate reviews conducted with professional assistance can reveal gaps or weaknesses in your plan, offering opportunities for refinement and enhancement. Regular reviews also account for changes in laws or regulations that might impact your estate, ensuring ongoing compliance and optimization. The support of professionals not only bolsters your plan's robustness but also provides peace of mind, knowing that your legacy is in capable hands.

Thorough documentation of your estate plan is crucial for clarity and execution. Without clear and detailed instructions, even the most well-intentioned plans can fall apart. Creating a comprehensive estate planning checklist helps organize your thoughts and ensures that no critical elements are overlooked. This checklist might include a list of assets, designated beneficiaries, and specific instructions for asset distribution. Organizing these documents securely is equally important. Consider a safe deposit box or a secure digital vault to store originals and copies. Make sure that your executor or trusted family members know where these documents are kept and how to access them when needed. Proper organization prevents confusion and delays, facilitating a smoother transition for your beneficiaries.

Planning for incapacitation and end-of-life decisions is an integral part of estate planning that often gets overlooked. It's essential to prepare for scenarios where you might be unable to make decisions due to illness or injury. Establishing powers of attorney ensures that someone you trust can manage your financial affairs if you become incapacitated. Similarly, healthcare directives outline your preferences for medical treatment, providing guidance to loved ones and healthcare providers during difficult times. These directives can include instructions on life-sustaining treatments, organ donation, and pain management. Discussing end-of-life care preferences with your family can be challenging but is necessary to ensure your wishes are respected. Open conversations about these topics can alleviate the emotional burden on your loved ones, providing clarity and comfort during an already stressful time.

As we conclude this chapter, remember that estate planning is an ongoing process, not a one-time event. By avoiding common mistakes, seeking professional guidance, and ensuring thorough documentation, you create a plan that reflects your intentions and adapts to life's changes. This proactive approach not only safeguards your legacy but also provides peace of mind for you and your loved ones. As we move forward, the next chapter will delve into managing debt and fixed income in retirement, providing strategies to maintain financial stability.

Don't move on to the next chapter without doing the following;

1. Do you have a will or trust? Please make sure you action this if you don't. It's really important and without one your estate gets managed by the state. Contact an estate attorney now
2. If you have a will or trusts when was it last updated? Do you need to update it?
3. Have you spoken to your family about your wishes and your will? Schedule this now
4. Put in your diary this time next year to review it again and see if anything needs updating
5. Do you have a power of attorney and a healthcare directive? Contact an attorney to draft this up

* * *

Make a Difference with Your Review

People who give without expecting anything in return live happier lives. So, let's make a difference together!

Would you help someone just like you—curious about Financial Freedom but unsure where to start?

My mission is to make Financial Freedom understandable for everyone. But to reach more people, I need your help. Most people choose books based on reviews. So, I'm asking you to help someone else by leaving a review.

It costs nothing and takes less than a minute but could change someone's financial journey and turn around a family's future. Your review could help...

...one more family get out of debt
  ...one parent build their emergency fund for their family
  ...one child understand money to start their life out better than they started
  ...one more person take control of their finances
  ...one more dream come true

To make a difference, simply scan the QR code below, or click on the link and leave a review:
  https://amzn.to/4a1Z8DH

Emma Maxwell

Chapter 7

Managing Debt and Fixed Income

Imagine standing at the threshold of retirement, a time meant for relaxation and the pursuit of passions, but instead, you're weighed down by financial obligations. You're not alone. Today, many retirees carry significant debt, a reality that was less common in previous generations. In fact, the percentage of households with an adult 65 or older carrying debt has risen sharply, with the average Baby Boomer shouldering approximately $90,000 in debt as of 2020. This chapter is dedicated to helping you manage and prioritize your debt repayment, ensuring that your retirement years are as worry-free as possible. By strategically addressing your debts, you can reclaim control over your finances and focus on enjoying your golden years.

7.1 Prioritizing Debt Repayment

The first step in tackling debt is taking a comprehensive inventory of your financial obligations. Begin by listing all your debts, including credit cards, mortgages, student loans, and any other outstanding balances. For each debt, note the current balance, interest rate, and monthly payment. Categorize them into secured debts, like mortgages, which are backed by collateral, and unsecured debts, such as credit cards, which aren't tied to an asset. This categorization helps you understand the full scope of your financial situation and identify which debts pose the greatest financial burden. By clearly seeing the details of your debts, you gain the insight necessary to formulate a plan for repayment.

With a clear picture of your debts, you can develop a strategic repayment plan that aligns with your financial situation and goals. Two popular methods for debt repayment are the Debt pay down method and the Debt accelerator method. The pay down method involves paying off debts from smallest to largest, gaining momentum as you eliminate each one. This approach provides a psychological boost, as the quick wins keep you motivated. On the other hand, the accelerator method focuses on paying off debts with the highest interest rates first, ultimately saving you more money in the long run. Each method has its merits, and the choice depends on your personal preferences and financial circumstances. Additionally, consider the pros and cons of consolidating high-interest debts into a single loan with a lower interest rate. Consolidation can simplify payments and potentially reduce interest costs, but it's essential to weigh the potential fees and ensure you don't accumulate new debt.

Reducing interest rates can significantly ease your debt burden, making repayment more manageable. Start by negotiating with creditors to lower your interest rates. Many creditors are open to discussions, especially if you have a history of timely payments. Call them, present your case clearly, highlighting your commitment to repaying the debt. Refinancing high-interest loans is another option. By securing a lower interest rate, you can reduce your monthly payments and the total interest paid over the life of the loan. However, refinancing often involves fees, so it's crucial to calculate the long-term savings to ensure it's a cost-effective move. Exploring these options can provide relief, allowing you to redirect more funds toward principal reduction.

Balancing debt repayment with saving for retirement is a delicate dance, but it's possible with careful planning. Setting dual goals for debt reduction and savings growth ensures you're not sacrificing your future for immediate relief. Reallocate any extra income, such as bonuses or tax refunds, toward both debt repayment and retirement savings. This approach maintains progress on both fronts, providing a sense of accomplishment and security. The ultimate aim should be to enter retirement debt-free, freeing your finances to focus on sustaining your lifestyle. While aggressive debt repayment is crucial, it's equally important to continue building your nest egg, ensuring you're prepared for the financial demands of retirement.

7.2 Strategies for Living on a Fixed Income

Living on a fixed income during retirement can feel like walking a tightrope. You have a set amount coming in each month, and it's up to you to ensure it stretches to cover all your needs. Unlike variable income, where earnings fluctuate and may increase over time, fixed income provides consistency but also limitations. Common sources include pensions, which are regular payments from previous employers, and annuities, contracts that pay out in a steady stream. These provide predictability, offering peace of mind, yet they also demand discipline in budgeting, as there's little room for unexpected expenses. Understanding these dynamics helps you plan with precision, ensuring your lifestyle aligns with your financial reality.

Maximizing government and retirement benefits is crucial to bolstering your fixed income. Social Security plays a vital role, and ensuring you receive full benefits can significantly impact your financial stability. This means being strategic about when to claim benefits. Delaying until age 70, for example, can increase your monthly check. Similarly, if you have a pension, verify its terms and explore any options to maximize payouts. Annuities also offer opportunities for optimization. Choosing the right payout option, whether it's a lifetime income or a fixed period, can affect your overall income. Each decision requires careful consideration of your long-term needs and financial goals, ensuring you're making the most of the benefits available to you.

If needed, adopting cost-saving measures is a practical approach to making your fixed income go further. Start by implementing energy-saving measures at home, such as using LED bulbs, sealing drafts, and setting your thermostat wisely. These small changes can lead to significant savings on utility bills. Additionally, take advantage of senior discounts available at many retailers, restaurants, and entertainment venues. These discounts can help reduce everyday costs, freeing up funds for other priorities. Community resources, like local libraries and senior centers, offer free or low-cost activities that provide enrichment without straining your budget. Living frugally doesn't mean sacrificing quality of life; it's about making thoughtful choices that align with your financial situation.

Planning for inflation and cost-of-living adjustments is essential to maintaining your purchasing power. Inflation can erode the value of your fixed income over time, making it crucial to incorporate strategies that protect against it. Investing in inflation-protected securities, like Treasury Inflation-Protected Securities (TIPS), can help preserve your wealth. These bonds increase in value with inflation, providing a hedge against rising costs. Moreover, it's important to adjust your budget annually to account for cost-of-living increases. This might mean reallocating funds from discretionary spending to cover essential expenses that have risen. By staying proactive and adaptable, you ensure that your income keeps pace with the changing economic landscape, maintaining the financial stability you've worked so hard to achieve. If you're finding that living on a fixed income is not enough for you to live on, you could consider pulling some funds from your retirement account to top up your income.

7.3 Creating a Retirement Budget

Crafting a realistic retirement budget is a vital step in safeguarding your financial stability during your golden years. This process begins by categorizing your expenses into fixed and discretionary categories. Fixed expenses, such as housing, utilities, and insurance, are predictable and recur monthly. These are your non-negotiables, the costs you must cover to maintain your standard of living. In contrast, discretionary expenses include things like dining out, travel, and hobbies. These are more flexible, offering opportunities for adjustments if your budget feels tight. Don't overlook irregular expenses— these are the surprises life throws your way, like a new car purchase or an unexpected home repair. Including these in your budget helps ensure you're prepared for life's unpredictabilities, reducing stress and financial strain.We created this in Chapter 1 & 4 but feel free to update it if things change.

To maintain a disciplined budgeting approach, consider implementing digital tools and apps designed for this purpose like we talked about in Chapter 1. Budgeting apps like Empower (formerly Personal Capital) and YNAB (You Need a Budget) offer comprehensive features that allow you to track expenses, set budget goals, and link directly to your bank accounts for seamless updates. These tools provide visual dashboards that clearly show where your money goes each month, making it easier to identify spending patterns and areas for improvement. The benefits of using digital tools extend beyond mere tracking. They offer insights and alerts that can help you stay on top of your finances, ensuring you stick to your plan and remain aligned with your retirement goals. By embracing technology, you gain a clearer view of your financial landscape, empowering you to make informed decisions.

As life evolves, so too should your budget. Regular reviews are crucial, allowing you to adjust for lifestyle changes and unexpected events. Consider scenario planning as a proactive approach, envisioning potential changes like moving to a different city, taking up a new hobby, or facing health-related expenses. This exercise helps you anticipate financial needs and reallocate funds within your budget accordingly. Techniques for reallocating might include shifting money from discretionary to fixed expenses or finding cost-saving opportunities in your daily routine. By staying flexible and adaptive, your budget can accommodate life's shifts without compromising your financial security.

Incorporating savings and emergency funds into your budget is another critical component. Setting aside a percentage of your income for savings ensures you're continually building a financial cushion, ready to support you in unforeseen circumstances. This might be as simple as a monthly transfer to a savings account or an automatic contribution to an investment fund. An emergency fund acts as your financial safety net, designed to cover unplanned expenses like medical emergencies or urgent home repairs. Building and maintaining this fund requires discipline, but it offers peace of mind, knowing you have resources to draw upon when needed. This should be in a money market account and easily accessible for expenses that may crop up. By integrating these elements into your budget, you create a comprehensive financial plan that supports both your current needs and future aspirations.

7.4 Managing Unexpected Expenses in Retirement

Retirement is often seen as a period of tranquility and enjoyment, but the reality can sometimes be jarring. Unanticipated expenses lurk around every corner, waiting to disrupt your peace. Imagine the sudden need for a major home repair, like a leaky roof that threatens to flood your living space, or the unexpected breakdown of your heating system in the dead of winter. These home repairs can quickly escalate into financial burdens if you're not prepared. Health-related expenses, which are not covered by insurance, can also take a hefty toll. Whether it's an unforeseen dental procedure or a medical emergency requiring out-of-pocket payments, these costs can strain a fixed income. Recognizing these potential pitfalls is the first step in safeguarding your financial health.

Creating a contingency plan for emergencies is akin to having a financial safety net. Establishing a separate contingency fund dedicated to unforeseen expenses ensures you're not caught off guard. This fund acts as your first line of defense, covering costs without dipping into your regular budget. The amount to set aside depends on your circumstances, but a good rule of thumb is to aim for three to six months worth of expenses. This cushion provides peace of mind, knowing you're prepared for whatever comes your way. In addition to building this fund, consider strategies for reallocating existing resources. If need be this might involve temporarily cutting back on discretionary spending or tapping into less critical savings to handle emergencies. By having a plan in place, you avoid the stress and potential financial chaos that unexpected events can bring.

Exploring insurance options is another critical strategy in mitigating the impact of significant unexpected financial burdens. Insurance policies like home warranties can cover the cost of major repairs, from appliances to plumbing, reducing your out-of-pocket expenses. Supplemental health insurance can fill gaps left by Medicare, covering services that might otherwise be unaffordable. When evaluating insurance options, consider the cost-benefit ratio carefully. Assess whether the premiums and deductibles align with your financial capacity and the likelihood of needing such coverage. It's essential to strike a balance between adequate protection and affordability. By choosing the right coverage, you protect your finances from potentially devastating expenses, ensuring your retirement remains financially secure.

Community resources and support offer invaluable assistance, especially for retirees. Local programs may provide aid in the form of subsidized home repairs, health services, or even financial advice. Senior centers often host workshops and seminars on managing finances, offering practical tips and strategies. Don't underestimate the power of community support networks, which can provide both financial and emotional support. Engaging with these resources not only helps you manage unexpected costs but also connects you with a community of peers facing similar challenges. Embracing available support can ease the burden of unforeseen expenses, allowing you to navigate retirement with confidence and grace.

As you consider the unpredictability of life, remember that preparation is key. Establishing contingency plans, exploring insurance options, and leveraging community resources are proactive steps that fortify your financial foundation. By anticipating and planning for the unexpected, you ensure that your retirement remains as stress-free and fulfilling as possible.

Exercise: Plan Your Retirement

Planning for retirement is more than just a financial exercise; it's about envisioning the life you want to lead and ensuring you have the resources to make it happen. Begin this process by listing all your potential income sources. These might include Social Security benefits, payouts from retirement funds, part-time work, or any other revenue streams. It's crucial to have a clear idea of your expected monthly or annual income, as this forms the foundation of your retirement plan. Think of this as mapping out your financial landscape, where each source of income acts as a pillar supporting your future lifestyle.

Next, turn your attention to expenses. You've already assessed your current costs in Chapter 1, but now it's time to project your future expenses. Consider which costs will diminish or disappear entirely in retirement. Will you have paid off your mortgage? Will commuting costs vanish as you step away from the workforce? Remember to account for inflation, which can significantly impact your purchasing power over time. Health care costs, long-term care fees, Medicare premiums, and any supplementary health insurance should also be factored in. These health-related expenses often become more prominent as we age, and planning for them is crucial to maintaining financial health. Compile a comprehensive list, ensuring no expense is overlooked, so you have a realistic view of what you'll need. If you didn't do this exercise in Chapter 1 & 4 do it now. The template you'll need is in Chapter 1.

One-off costs require special attention. These are the larger, less frequent expenditures that can disrupt your budget if unplanned. Think about setting aside funds for a healthcare emergency fund, home maintenance or upgrades, purchasing a new car, or even planning vacations. These costs are like the unexpected plot twists in a novel; they can catch you off guard if you're not prepared. By forecasting these expenses and incorporating them into your financial plan, you ensure that they don't become financial burdens. This foresight allows you to enjoy life's surprises rather than fear them, providing peace of mind in your retirement years.

Once you have your lists, input this information into an online retirement calculator like Boldin. Websites like Vanguard or Fidelity offer user-friendly retirement calculators to help you calculate your "retirement number"—the amount you'll need to sustain your lifestyle. These calculators consider factors like inflation, investment returns, and life expectancy, providing a personalized snapshot of your financial future. The result is a clear target to aim for, highlighting any gaps between your current savings and future needs. If your retirement number is alarmingly different from your current savings, it's time to strategize. Consider adjusting your risk profile, perhaps shifting to investments with higher returns if you're comfortable with the increased risk. Consult with your HR department or an investment advisor, or login online to your funds portal to explore funds with better performance and lower fees. Reducing expenses and exploring ways to increase your income, such as part-time work or side projects, can also help bridge the gap.

As you conclude this exercise, remember that retirement planning is an ongoing process, not a one-time task. It requires regular revisiting and adjusting as your circumstances and the economic landscape evolve. This proactive approach ensures that you're not just planning for retirement but actively shaping a future that aligns with your dreams and goals. With a solid plan in place, you're well-equipped to transition into the next chapter of your life, confident in your financial security and ready to embrace the opportunities that come your way.

Don't move on to the next chapter without doing the following;

1. List out your debts and have a plan in place to pay them down
2. Create or review your retirement budget. If you didn't do it already, do that now
3. Calculate your retirement number in either Boldin or using an online retirement calculator like Vanguard

Chapter 8

Emotional and Psychological Preparation

Approaching retirement can feel like standing on the edge of a vast, unknown territory, filled with both promise and uncertainty. For many, the transition from a structured work life to a more fluid routine can stir up a whirlwind of emotions. It's a period marked by significant change, where the familiar rhythm of daily tasks gives way to uncharted freedom. This chapter addresses the emotional and psychological shifts that accompany retirement, offering insights and strategies to navigate this new stage of life with confidence and clarity. Understanding these changes is crucial, as it sets the stage for a fulfilling and balanced retirement.

8.1 Understanding the Emotional Impact of Retirement

Retirement often heralds a profound shift in one's sense of identity and purpose. After years of defining ourselves through our careers, stepping away can lead to feelings of loss. Many retirees find themselves asking, "Who am I without my job?" This question can evoke a deep sense of uncertainty. The daily interactions with colleagues, the structure of a workday, and the sense of contribution to a larger goal provide a framework that many miss.

It's common to feel adrift, as though a key part of one's identity has been left behind. This loss of identity can lead to emotional struggles, including anxiety and even depression, as one grapples with redefining their place in the world.

The financial aspect of retirement also plays a significant role in emotional well-being. Concerns about financial security can overshadow the excitement of newfound freedom. The transition from a regular paycheck to managing a fixed income requires careful planning and adjustment. Many retirees worry about whether they have enough savings to sustain their lifestyle, contributing to anxiety and stress. This financial uncertainty can affect mental health, creating a cycle of worry that overshadows the potential joys of retirement. Addressing these concerns and developing a realistic financial plan can alleviate some of these fears, allowing you to focus on enjoying this new chapter.

The psychological shift from a structured work environment to a more open-ended lifestyle is another crucial aspect to consider. The workplace often provides a routine and sense of purpose that can be hard to replicate in retirement. Without a set schedule, there can be a loss of daily structure, leading to feelings of aimlessness. The freedom to manage your own time may sound appealing, but it requires self-discipline and motivation to create a fulfilling schedule. Establishing a new routine that incorporates activities, social interaction, and personal growth can offer a sense of stability and purpose. This self-directed time management is key to a successful transition, helping to replace the structure that work once provided.

Understanding the stages of emotional adjustment during retirement can be likened to a cycle similar to grief. Initially, there may be a sense of excitement and relief as you embrace the freedom from work-related stresses. However, this can be followed by a period of disillusionment as the reality of retirement sets in. It's normal to feel a sense of loss and uncertainty during this phase. Gradually, though, acceptance and adaptation emerge, as you begin to redefine your identity and establish new routines. This gradual acceptance is a critical part of the adjustment process, signaling a shift towards embracing the opportunities that retirement offers. Recognizing these stages helps in acknowledging that emotional ups and downs are a natural part of the transition.

Coping with the emotional challenges of retirement requires practical strategies to manage and work through these feelings. Journaling can be an effective tool for processing emotions and thoughts, providing a private space to explore concerns and aspirations. Regular writing can help clarify feelings and offer insights into personal growth. Mindfulness and meditation practices are also valuable, as they promote relaxation and reduce stress. These practices encourage living in the moment, helping to calm the mind and focus on the present. Connecting with others, especially fellow retirees, can provide support and shared understanding. Engaging in conversations with those who are experiencing similar transitions can offer comfort and perspective. Whether through informal gatherings or support groups, these connections remind you that you are not alone in this journey.

Reflection Section: Navigating Emotional Adjustments

Consider the following questions as you reflect on your emotional preparation for retirement:

- How do you define your identity beyond your career?
- What financial concerns do you have, and how can you address them?
- What new routines can you establish to provide structure and purpose?
- How will you navigate the stages of emotional adjustment, from excitement to acceptance?
- What strategies will you employ to cope with emotional challenges?

Reflecting on these questions can guide your path, ensuring that you embrace this new phase with resilience and optimism.

8.2 Finding Purpose and Fulfillment

Retirement opens up a world of possibilities, offering time to explore interests long placed on the back burner. It's a chance to dive into hobbies and pursuits that once seemed out of reach. Imagine the satisfaction of engaging in lifelong learning through classes or workshops. Whether it's pottery, photography, or even a new language, these activities stimulate the mind and nurture creativity. Creative pursuits like painting or writing not only keep your hands busy but also allow you to express emotions and ideas. They become a source of joy and fulfillment, providing both a creative outlet and a sense of achievement. Embracing new interests can transform your days, filling them with purpose and excitement. This exploration of interests is not just about filling time; it's about enriching your life and discovering passions that truly resonate with you.

Volunteering is another avenue that offers immense personal satisfaction and a sense of purpose. By giving back to the community, you create meaningful connections and contribute to causes that matter. Opportunities abound in local charities and non-profits, where your skills and experience can make a real difference. From assisting at food banks to helping at animal shelters, the options are diverse and rewarding. Mentorship programs present another fulfilling path, allowing you to guide younger generations, sharing wisdom accumulated over years of experience. It's an opportunity to leave a lasting impact, nurturing the growth and development of others. And if you're not ready to completely step away from the workforce, part-time work or consulting can bridge the gap. It provides not only an income stream but also keeps you engaged and connected to your professional identity, offering a balanced approach to retirement.

Setting personal goals is crucial for maintaining a sense of direction and motivation. Creating a bucket list of experiences or achievements can serve as a road map for this new chapter. Perhaps there are places you've always dreamed of visiting or skills you've longed to master. These aspirations add excitement and anticipation to your days, providing clear targets to strive for. Health and wellness objectives are equally important, ensuring that you maintain physical vitality and mental clarity. Whether it's committing to a regular exercise routine or adopting healthier eating habits, these goals support a balanced lifestyle. They reinforce the notion that retirement is not a time of decline but a period for growth and renewal. By aligning these goals with your passions and values, you create a fulfilling and purposeful retirement, filled with opportunities for personal development and enrichment.

Consider the stories of retirees who have successfully found new purpose, each offering inspiration and insight. Take, for example, a retired engineer who discovered a passion for woodworking, transforming a hobby into a business that crafts bespoke furniture for the community. His journey highlights the potential to reinvent oneself, turning skills into new ventures. Another retiree found joy in volunteering at a local school, where she tutors children in reading. Her efforts not only improve literacy but also foster a love for learning, impacting the lives of countless students. These stories illustrate the myriad of ways retirees can contribute, finding fulfillment in sharing their talents and knowledge with others. They remind us that retirement is not an end but a beginning, a time to embrace new roles and make meaningful contributions to society. Each narrative underscores the power of purpose, demonstrating how it enriches both the individual and the community.

Case Study: The Power of New Beginnings

Meet John, a former corporate executive who spent decades climbing the career ladder. Upon retiring, he felt a void, unsure how to fill the hours once dedicated to work. Urged by a friend, he attended a local art class, discovering a latent talent for painting. As he honed his skills, John's confidence grew, leading to his first public exhibition. Encouraged by positive feedback, he now teaches art classes, sharing his newfound passion with others. John's story exemplifies the transformative power of exploring new interests in retirement. It shows how stepping outside your comfort zone can unveil hidden talents and open doors to unexpected opportunities. His journey is a testament to the endless possibilities that retirement offers, inspiring others to pursue their passions and find fulfillment in uncharted territories of creativity and self-expression.

8.3 Building a Supportive Retirement Network

As you transition into retirement, the importance of a strong support network cannot be overstated. Maintaining social connections is vital for emotional well-being and can significantly enhance the quality of your retirement years. Existing friendships and family ties offer a familiar foundation, providing comfort and reassurance. These relationships remind you that you're not alone as you navigate this new phase of life. They offer a sense of belonging, a safe space to share your experiences, and a source of encouragement when exploring new interests or facing challenges. Cherish these ties and nurture them, as they are the anchors that keep you grounded.

For many, support groups tailored to retirees offer another layer of connection. These groups bring together individuals experiencing similar transitions, providing a platform for shared understanding and empathy. They offer a space to discuss feelings, exchange advice, and gain insights from others who have walked the same path. Participating in such groups can alleviate feelings of isolation, fostering a sense of community and camaraderie. Whether through formal meetings or informal gatherings, these connections enrich your social life and provide emotional sustenance.

Expanding your social circle during retirement is equally important. It opens up opportunities to meet new people and form fresh friendships that can add vibrancy to your daily life. Joining clubs or groups based on shared interests, such as gardening, book clubs, or hiking, creates natural conversation starters and common ground, making it easier to connect with others. These activities not only stimulate your mind but also foster a sense of belonging, as you engage with like-minded individuals. Participating in community events and activities is another excellent way to widen your social network. Whether it's attending local festivals, volunteering at community centers, or joining fitness classes, these activities introduce you to new faces and experiences, enhancing your retirement lifestyle.

In today's digital age, technology plays a crucial role in maintaining and expanding social connections. Video calls and social media platforms keep you connected with loved ones, regardless of distance. They allow you to share moments, celebrate milestones, and maintain meaningful relationships with family and friends. Online platforms such as Meetup or Eventbrite can help you discover local events and interest groups, providing opportunities to meet new people in your area. These digital tools bridge the gap between physical distance and social interaction, ensuring you remain connected and engaged.

However, social interactions in retirement can present challenges, particularly if you're naturally shy or reserved. Overcoming social anxieties involves developing strategies to initiate conversations and form new relationships. Begin by practicing active listening, showing genuine interest in others, and asking open-ended questions that encourage dialogue. This approach helps you build confidence and fosters deeper connections. If shyness or social withdrawal is a barrier, start with small steps. Attend events with a friend for support or choose gatherings that align with your interests, where you're more likely to feel comfortable. Gradually, as you engage more with others, your confidence will grow, allowing you to embrace new social opportunities.

In retirement, the value of a strong support network becomes clear. It nurtures emotional well-being, enriches your daily experiences, and provides a sense of community. By maintaining existing ties, expanding your social circle, and utilizing technology, you create a vibrant social landscape that supports your journey through retirement. Addressing social anxieties and embracing new relationships ensures that your retirement years are filled with connection, joy, and fulfillment, empowering you to navigate this life stage with confidence and grace.

Don't forget to plan things with and without your spouse. You aren't used to spending 24x7 together so it's important to do things together but also have some time apart. Communicating your boundaries and preferences enables your relationship in retirement to thrive.

8.4 Overcoming Retirement Anxiety

Retirement, a phase eagerly anticipated by many, can also be a source of significant anxiety. This is a time when concerns about financial stability often come to the forefront. The fear of outliving your savings is a common anxiety, especially if you haven't had the chance to save as much as you'd hoped. This fear can cast a long shadow, making it difficult to enjoy the freedom that retirement should bring. It's essential to address these financial worries head-on, possibly by revisiting your retirement plan or consulting with a financial advisor to ensure your savings will support your lifestyle. These discussions can provide much-needed reassurance, helping to mitigate some of the anxiety surrounding your financial future.

Uncertainty about health and longevity is another prevalent source of retirement anxiety. As we age, the unpredictability of health becomes more apparent, and it's natural to worry about potential health issues. In retirement, when you're no longer covered by employer health plans, these concerns can feel even more pressing. It's important to have a solid healthcare plan in place, including Medicare or other supplemental insurances. Knowing your health coverage options and planning for potential medical expenses can alleviate some of the stress associated with health uncertainties. Also, consider discussing these concerns with your partner, if you have one. They may be experiencing similar fears, and sharing your worries can foster mutual support and understanding, creating a stronger partnership as you both navigate this new stage of life.

Implementing stress-reduction techniques is crucial for managing retirement anxiety. Simple practices like breathing exercises and progressive muscle relaxation can help reduce immediate stress. These techniques encourage you to focus on the present moment, calming your mind and body. Regular physical activity is another powerful tool for stress management. Exercise releases endorphins, which boost mood and reduce stress, while also contributing to overall physical well-being. Whether it's walking, swimming, or yoga, find an activity you enjoy and make it a regular part of your routine.

These practices not only help manage anxiety but also enhance your quality of life during retirement, providing both physical and mental health benefits that contribute to a fulfilling lifestyle.

The role of professional support in managing retirement anxiety should not be underestimated. Seeking help from a therapist, especially one who specializes in retirement transitions, can provide invaluable support. Therapy offers a safe space to explore your anxieties and develop coping strategies tailored to your needs. Cognitive-behavioral therapy (CBT), in particular, is effective for managing anxiety. It helps you identify and change negative thought patterns, promoting a more positive outlook on retirement. Engaging in therapy can provide clarity and peace of mind, equipping you with the tools to tackle retirement challenges head-on. Professional support can be a cornerstone in building a healthy, balanced retirement, offering guidance and insight as you navigate this significant life change.

Developing a proactive mindset is another key aspect of overcoming retirement anxiety. Adopting a positive and proactive approach helps you manage change with confidence and resilience. Practicing gratitude is a simple yet powerful way to shift your focus from anxiety to appreciation, highlighting the positive aspects of your life. Take time each day to reflect on what you're grateful for, whether it's the freedom to pursue new interests or the support of loved ones. Setting small, achievable goals can also build confidence and momentum, providing a sense of accomplishment and progress. These goals need not be grand; they could be as simple as learning a new skill or completing a home project. By focusing on the positives and celebrating small victories, you cultivate a mindset that embraces change, turning retirement into an opportunity for growth and fulfillment.

As you embrace this new chapter, remember that retirement is not just an end but a beginning filled with potential. Addressing sources of anxiety, implementing stress-reduction techniques, seeking professional support, and developing a proactive mindset can transform your retirement experience. By approaching this stage with curiosity and openness, you pave the way for a vibrant and fulfilling retirement. With these strategies in place, you are well-equipped to face the future with confidence, ensuring that your retirement years are rich with joy, purpose, and peace.

Don't move on to the next chapter without doing the following;

1. Plan your ideal retirement day - share this with your spouse
2. Research aspects of your ideal day above and look at groups or classes you can join to implement these things
3. What have you always wanted to do that now that you have more time you could do? Why wait, make it happen
4. What groups can you join to expand your social circle?

Chapter 9

Future-Proofing Your Retirement

Imagine you're embarking on a new adventure, a journey through retirement that promises both freedom and uncertainty. You stand on the precipice of this new chapter, armed with dreams and plans, yet you're aware that the road ahead is uncharted. One of the most significant challenges you'll face is the risk of outliving your savings. This longevity risk is not just a possibility—it's a growing reality for many. As medical advancements continue and lifestyles evolve, people are living longer than previous generations. According to the CDC, the average life expectancy in the United States is now 77.5 years, with women living to 80.2 years on average, and men to 74.8 years. These numbers underscore the necessity of preparing for a potentially extended retirement period, where your financial resources must stretch further than you might have initially anticipated.

Living longer presents both challenges and opportunities. On one hand, an extended lifespan means more time to enjoy the fruits of your labor, travel, spend time with family, and pursue passions. On the other hand, it brings increased pressure on your financial resources. Healthcare costs are likely to rise as you age, with expenses for medication, treatments, and potentially long-term care becoming significant burdens. The impact of longevity on your living expenses cannot be underestimated. The longer you live, the more you'll need to allocate for daily living expenses, healthcare, and unexpected costs. This reality makes it crucial to evaluate whether your current retirement savings are adequate. It's not enough to save for twenty years of retirement when you might live thirty or more. This shift in perspective is vital to ensure that you maintain your quality of life throughout your golden years.

Assessing the adequacy of your retirement savings requires a thorough and honest evaluation of your financial situation. Begin by using calculators designed to project longevity-adjusted retirement needs. Tools like the Retirement Planner app and Boldin can help you compare projections and understand how your savings will support you over an extended period. These calculators consider factors such as inflation, expected lifespan, and current savings rates to provide a clearer picture of your financial future. Adjusting your withdrawal rates is another critical component. Withdrawing too much too soon can deplete your savings, leaving you vulnerable in your later years. A common strategy is the "4% rule," which suggests withdrawing 4% of your retirement savings annually, adjusting for inflation which at a high level means your savings last for 25 years. However, this rule may need tweaking based on your personal circumstances, health, and market conditions.

Exploring annuities and lifetime income solutions is another effective strategy to mitigate longevity risk. Annuities are financial products that provide a steady income stream for life, offering peace of mind that you won't outlive your resources. There are various types of annuities to consider. Immediate annuities begin payments almost immediately after purchase, providing quick income. Deferred annuities, on the other hand, start payments at a future date, allowing your investment to grow in the meantime. Each type has its merits, depending on your financial needs and timing preferences. Longevity insurance, a specific type of annuity, kicks in at an advanced age, such as 85, ensuring you receive income when other resources might be exhausted. While annuities can offer security, they also come with drawbacks. They can be complex and costly, often involving fees that can eat into your returns. It's essential to weigh these pros and cons carefully, considering your overall financial picture and consulting a financial advisor if needed.

Alongside financial strategies, maintaining health and wellness plays a pivotal role in enhancing your quality of life in later years. A healthy lifestyle can reduce healthcare costs and contribute to a longer, more active life. Regular exercise is fundamental, promoting cardiovascular health, flexibility, and mental well-being. Whether it's walking, swimming, or yoga; find an activity you enjoy and can sustain long-term. Coupled with exercise, a balanced diet rich in nutrients supports your overall health. Emphasize whole foods, lean proteins, and plenty of fruits and vegetables, and stay hydrated. Preventive healthcare measures are equally important. Regular check-ups and screenings can catch potential health issues early, reducing the risk of costly medical interventions later. Vaccinations, dental care, and eye exams should also be part of your routine health maintenance.

Reflection Section: Longevity and Lifestyle

Take a moment to consider how longevity might influence your retirement. Reflect on these questions to help guide your planning:

- How might extended longevity impact your current retirement savings strategy?
- Are there adjustments you need to make to your withdrawal rates to ensure your savings last?
- Have you explored annuities or other lifetime income products as part of your financial plan?
- What steps can you take now to maintain and improve your health, potentially lowering future healthcare costs?
- How do your lifestyle choices today affect your long-term quality of life and financial security?

By considering these aspects, you can better prepare for the future, ensuring that your retirement remains secure and fulfilling.

9.1 Embracing Technology in Retirement Planning

As you approach retirement, technology can be your steadfast ally, streamlining the complex processes of planning and managing your financial future. In today's digital age, a plethora of financial planning apps and software are at your fingertips, ready to transform how you approach retirement savings. These tools range from simple budgeting apps to sophisticated platforms offering comprehensive investment management. Apps like the Retirement Planner and Boldin help you visualize your future finances by projecting retirement income based on different savings scenarios. They provide clarity, showing how your current savings and contributions align with your retirement goals. For more advanced management, robo-advisors like Betterment or Wealthfront offer automated investment services. They build and manage your portfolio using algorithms, often at a lower cost than traditional financial advisors. These digital platforms assess your risk tolerance, financial goals, and timeline to craft a personalized investment strategy, adjusting as markets fluctuate. With these tools, you gain a clearer picture of your financial landscape, enabling informed decisions about your retirement.

Beyond financial management, technology opens doors to continuous learning and community engagement, vital components of a successful retirement plan. The internet is a treasure trove of educational resources, offering webinars and online courses designed to enhance your financial literacy. Websites like Coursera and Udemy provide free or affordable courses on topics ranging from basic budgeting to advanced investment strategies. Engaging in these courses expands your knowledge and equips you with the skills to navigate the financial intricacies of retirement. Meanwhile, online forums and communities such as Reddit's retirement subreddits or personal finance groups on Facebook foster interaction and support. These platforms connect you with others on a similar path, enabling you to share experiences, ask questions, and receive advice from peers and experts alike. This sense of community can be reassuring, offering insights and encouragement as you plan for the future.

With the rise of digital tools comes the increased need to protect your digital assets and personal information. Strong password practices are your first line of defense. Use complex passwords that combine letters, numbers, and symbols, and avoid using the same password across multiple sites. Consider using a password manager to keep track of your credentials securely. Two-factor authentication adds another layer of security, requiring a secondary form of identification beyond just a password. This could be a code sent to your phone or a fingerprint scan, providing an additional safeguard against unauthorized access. As you build your digital presence, creating a digital estate plan becomes crucial. This plan ensures your digital assets - such as online accounts, social media profiles, and digital subscriptions - are managed according to your wishes in the event of incapacitation or death. Document your digital assets, appoint a digital executor, and provide instructions on how to access and manage these accounts. This forward-thinking approach protects your digital legacy and provides peace of mind for you and your loved ones.

Be careful with scams on email or online asking you to click on links or enter in your credit card or banking information. These emails look so legitimate it's easy to be fooled but just exercise caution when anyone is asking for this information. Also be weary when transferring large amounts of cash that you have verbally confirmed the bank account details with the person you're transferring to. I've seen too many people lose money to not re-iterate it to you here.

Technological advancements extend beyond financial planning, revolution-izing healthcare access and management. Telemedicine services have become increasingly popular, offering virtual consultations with healthcare providers from the comfort of your home. These services are convenient, eliminating travel time and providing access to specialists who may not be available locally. Virtual health consultations allow for ongoing health monitoring, prescription renewals, and even diagnosis of minor ailments, all through a secure online platform. Wearable health devices, such as fitness trackers and smartwatches, offer real-time monitoring of vital signs like heart rate, sleep patterns, and physical activity levels. These devices empower you to take control of your health, providing insights that can inform lifestyle choices and medical decisions. They also facilitate remote monitoring by healthcare providers, ensuring you receive timely interventions without the need for frequent in-person visits. By embracing these innovations, you enhance your healthcare experience, maintaining both independence and well-being as you age.

Incorporating these technological tools into your retirement planning not only simplifies financial management but also enriches your overall lifestyle. The digital world offers a wealth of resources to support your goals, from financial literacy and community engagement to security measures and health management. Embracing technology empowers you to take charge of your retirement journey, ensuring you remain informed, connected, and prepared for whatever the future holds.

9.2 Adapting to Evolving Financial Products

Navigating the financial landscape as you approach retirement can feel like trying to hit a moving target. New investment vehicles and financial products are constantly emerging, each promising to enhance your portfolio or offer unique benefits. Staying informed about these developments is crucial. Exchange-Traded Funds (ETFs), for instance, have become a popular choice for many investors due to their flexibility and typically lower fees compared to mutual funds. They allow you to invest in a broad array of asset classes, providing diversification that can help mitigate risk. Real Estate Investment Trusts (REITs) offer another avenue, enabling you to invest in real estate without the need to buy property directly. These trusts pay dividends and can be a stable income source, especially in retirement. Understanding these products can help you make informed decisions that align with your retirement goals and risk tolerance.

In recent years, blockchain technology and cryptocurrency have also entered the financial arena, offering both promise and complexity. Cryptocurrencies like Bitcoin and Ethereum have captured headlines with their dramatic price swings and potential for high returns. However, they are also notorious for their volatility and risk. Blockchain, the technology underpinning cryptocurrencies, is seen by many as transformative, providing transparency and security in financial transactions. As you consider these new opportunities, it's important to evaluate their suitability for your retirement portfolio. Consider the risk versus reward, your own comfort with uncertainty, and how these investments fit within your broader financial strategy. Knowledge is power, and understanding the intricacies of these products can help you navigate the choppy waters of modern finance.

Assessing new financial products requires a careful approach. Begin by examining the criteria for evaluating investment opportunities. Look for factors such as historical performance, management fees, and market trends. Assess the liquidity of the investment—how easily it can be bought or sold without affecting its price. Consider the tax implications and how they might impact your overall financial picture. Risk assessment is another key component. While high-risk investments can offer substantial returns, they also come with the potential for significant losses. Align any new investments with your risk tolerance, ensuring they complement rather than complicate your existing portfolio. Seeking advice from financial professionals can provide an additional layer of insight. Financial advisors can offer tailored guidance, helping you weigh the pros and cons of each investment and how it aligns with your personal goals.

Leveraging flexible financial products can provide adaptability in the face of life's uncertainties. Hybrid life insurance policies, for example, combine life insurance with long-term care riders. These products offer the dual benefit of a death benefit and coverage for long-term care expenses, should you need it. This flexibility can be invaluable, providing peace of mind that your needs will be met, regardless of how your life unfolds. Flexible spending accounts (FSAs) and health savings accounts (HSAs) are another way to adapt to changing circumstances. FSAs allow you to set aside pre-tax dollars for eligible healthcare expenses, reducing your taxable income and providing a financial cushion for medical costs. HSAs offer similar benefits, with funds that roll over year to year, making them a valuable tool for long-term health expense planning. These products offer the ability to adjust and respond to life's changes, ensuring you're prepared for whatever comes your way.

Consulting with financial advisors can be a wise move as you navigate this complex landscape. Advisors bring a wealth of knowledge and experience, helping you make sense of new products and determine their relevance to your retirement plan. They can assist in evaluating investment strategies, ensuring they align with your risk tolerance and financial goals. I do suggest going to a fee based advisor as then they won't be trying to sell you products from their portfolio and they have your best interests at heart when they make their recommendation. Regular financial reviews with a professional can offer fresh perspectives, highlighting areas for improvement or adjustment. These reviews ensure your strategy remains dynamic, adapting to market conditions and personal changes. The benefits of periodic financial check-ups extend beyond immediate gains, fostering a long-term approach that secures your financial future. While the financial world is ever-evolving, staying informed and adaptable ensures you remain in control, ready to seize opportunities and navigate challenges with confidence.

9.3 Anticipating Future Economic Changes

In the world of retirement planning, understanding economic indicators is like having a compass in your financial toolkit. These indicators, such as Gross Domestic Product (GDP), inflation rates, and interest rates, serve as vital signals that can affect your financial decisions. GDP reflects the overall economic health, showing whether an economy is growing or shrinking. A growing GDP often signals a robust economy, which can lead to higher stock market returns, while a shrinking GDP might indicate economic challenges. Inflation rates, on the other hand, measure the pace at which prices for goods and services rise, affecting purchasing power. High inflation can erode retirement savings, making it crucial to invest in products that keep pace with or outpace inflation. Interest rates determine the cost of borrowing money and the return on savings. When rates rise, it can mean higher returns on savings accounts but also more expensive loans. Historical analysis of economic cycles shows that economies go through periods of expansion and contraction. By understanding these cycles, you can better anticipate changes and adjust your retirement planning accordingly.

Preparing for market volatility and economic downturns is another critical aspect of safeguarding your retirement. Diversification is a powerful technique to minimize market risk. By spreading investments across various asset classes, such as stocks, bonds, and real estate, you reduce the impact of a poor-performing investment on your overall portfolio. This approach prevents you from being overly reliant on any single investment or sector, providing a cushion during economic turbulence. Creating a financial buffer, such as an emergency fund, is equally important. This reserve should cover at least 3 to 6 months of living expenses, allowing you to manage unexpected financial setbacks without dipping into your retirement savings. During downturns, having this buffer ensures you can maintain your lifestyle and avoid liquidating investments at a loss. By preparing for volatility, you create a resilient financial strategy capable of weathering economic storms.

Adjusting your financial strategies for inflation and deflation is essential to maintaining the purchasing power of your retirement income. Inflation can significantly devalue your savings over time, so it's crucial to invest in assets that hedge against it. Treasury Inflation-Protected Securities (TIPS) are a popular choice, as they adjust with inflation, ensuring your investment keeps pace with rising prices. Real estate and commodities also provide a hedge, as their values often increase with inflation. Conversely, deflation, a decrease in prices, can also impact your retirement income. During deflationary periods, cash and fixed-income investments may become more valuable as the purchasing power of money increases. Understanding how inflation and deflation affect your retirement finances allows you to adjust your portfolio to protect your wealth. By doing so, you ensure your financial plan remains robust, regardless of economic conditions.

Embracing a proactive and adaptable mindset is key to navigating the ever-changing economic landscape. Regularly reviewing and updating your financial plans ensures they align with current conditions and your evolving goals. Life events, market changes and unexpected circumstances can all necessitate adjustments to your retirement strategy. Building adaptability into your financial decision-making processes involves being open to change and willing to explore new opportunities. This might mean reallocating assets, adjusting withdrawal rates, or even considering new investment vehicles. By staying informed and flexible, you position yourself to make strategic choices that enhance your financial security. This proactive approach not only protects your retirement savings but also empowers you to seize opportunities that arise from economic shifts.

In summary, anticipating future economic changes involves understanding key indicators, preparing for volatility, and adjusting strategies for inflation and deflation. By staying informed and adaptable, you ensure your retirement remains stable and secure. As we move forward, we'll explore how these strategies integrate into a holistic retirement plan, ensuring a future that's both financially and personally fulfilling.

Don't move on to the next chapter without doing the following;

1. Create a Boldin or Retirement Planner account and log in and fill in your information from Chapters 1 & 4 using the Income and Expenses budget we created. Add your retirement age, Social Security full retirement age (FRA) and the age you plan to live to and see what that does to your retirement savings

2. Explore whether annuities are of interest to you in your retirement portfolio

3. Do you need to improve your health? What's your plan to make that happen?

4. Do you need to meet with a fee only financial advisor to help plan your portfolio? Book it in

Chapter 10

Living a Fulfilling Retirement

Imagine waking up each day with the freedom to fill it with activities that bring joy, purpose, and satisfaction. This is the essence of a fulfilling retirement. It's a time when you can finally indulge in the passions you've always dreamed of, without the constraints of a work schedule. But to truly enjoy this newfound freedom, balancing leisure with financial prudence is key. A fulfilling retirement isn't about lavish spending; it's about making thoughtful choices that allow you to enjoy life while ensuring financial security and longevity. This chapter will guide you through finding that balance, so you can savor the pleasures of retirement without financial worry.

10.1 Balancing Leisure and Financial Prudence

In retirement, leisure activities are vital for maintaining happiness and well-being, yet they must be approached with a sense of fiscal responsibility. Setting a realistic budget for leisure activities helps ensure that your enjoyment does not compromise financial security. Begin by assessing your monthly income and expenses, allocating a portion specifically for leisure. This budget should reflect your financial comfort zone, allowing room for spontaneity while keeping broader financial goals in check. Identifying cost-effective entertainment options can further enhance this balance. Consider matinee shows, community theater, or local art exhibits, which often provide cultural enrichment at a fraction of the cost. By planning thoughtfully, you can indulge in leisure activities without overextending your finances.

Prioritizing experiences over material possessions can greatly enhance your retirement satisfaction. Experiences create lasting memories and emotional connections, offering more profound fulfillment than transient material goods. Plan experience-based gifts for family and friends, such as concert tickets or a day at a local museum. These gifts foster shared moments and strengthen relationships. Creating a list of desired experiences to pursue can serve as a road map for your retirement adventures. Whether it's learning to sail or attending a wine tasting, these experiences enrich your life and provide stories to share for years to come. Focusing on experiences encourages meaningful living, turning each day into an opportunity for joy and discovery.

Exploring free or low-cost activities can lead to unexpected delights. Many communities offer sponsored events and festivals that are both entertaining and budget-friendly. From outdoor concerts to cultural fairs, these events provide opportunities to engage with your community and explore local culture. Nature-based activities like hiking or bird watching offer the dual benefits of exercise and relaxation, all at minimal cost. These pursuits encourage you to appreciate the beauty around you and provide a sense of peace and connection with the natural world. By seeking out these opportunities, you can fill your days with enriching experiences that don't strain your wallet.

Integrating leisure into your daily routine is essential for a balanced retirement life. Schedule regular hobbies and interests to ensure they are a consistent part of your week. Whether it's a morning walk, an afternoon of painting, or an evening of reading, dedicating time to these activities helps maintain a sense of purpose and structure. Setting aside time for relaxation and reflection is equally important. This might involve a quiet moment in your garden or a meditative practice like yoga. These moments of solitude allow you to recharge and reflect on your experiences, fostering a deeper appreciation for the life you've created. By weaving leisure into your routine, you create a tapestry of joy and fulfillment that enhances every day.

Reflection Section: Crafting Your Leisure Budget

Take a moment to reflect on how you can balance leisure and financial prudence:

- **Budgeting for Leisure:** What portion of your monthly income can you comfortably allocate to leisure activities?
- **Experience Prioritization:** What experiences do you value most, and how can you plan to incorporate them into your retirement?
- **Cost-Effective Options:** What free or low-cost activities are available in your community that align with your interests?
- **Daily Integration:** How can you incorporate leisure activities into your routine to ensure they are a regular part of your life?

Reflecting on these questions can help you create a retirement filled with joy and financial security, allowing you to savor every moment.

10.2 Exploring New Hobbies and Interests

Retirement presents a unique opportunity to venture into new territories of personal expression and joy. Encouraging the discovery of new passions can inject a sense of vitality and excitement into your daily life. Joining hobbyist clubs or groups is a wonderful starting point. These communities not only provide guidance for beginners but also foster a sense of camaraderie among like-minded individuals. Whether it's a local gardening club or an online art forum, these groups can become a part of your social fabric, offering both encouragement and inspiration. Experimenting with artistic endeavors, such as painting or music, can be particularly rewarding. Not only do these activities allow you to express yourself creatively, but they also provide a soothing retreat from the everyday hustle. Imagine picking up a brush and losing yourself in vibrant colors, or strumming a few chords to create a melody that resonates with your soul. These experiences can be deeply fulfilling and offer a profound sense of accomplishment.

Hobbies do more than fill your time; they enhance your mental well-being and provide a profound sense of fulfillment. Engaging in hobbies activates the brain, offering cognitive benefits that keep your mind sharp and agile. Learning new skills challenges the brain, fostering neuroplasticity and improving memory. Additionally, these activities often lead to social connections that enrich your life. Shared interests can bridge new friendships, creating bonds that offer support and joy. Whether it's through a local knitting circle or a community theater group, these relationships can transform your social landscape, providing laughter, companionship, and shared memories. Such interactions are invaluable, creating a sense of belonging and community that enriches your retirement years.

Getting started with new hobbies might feel daunting, but with practical guidance, you can overcome initial hurdles. Begin by exploring resources for finding local classes or workshops in your area. Libraries, community centers, and local colleges often offer courses that cater to varied interests. If in-person classes aren't feasible, online platforms provide a wealth of tutorials and guides, allowing you to learn at your own pace. Websites like YouTube or Skillshare offer extensive libraries of instructional videos, covering everything from basic guitar chords to advanced photography techniques. These resources make learning accessible and enjoyable, breaking down complex skills into manageable steps. With a bit of curiosity and willingness, you'll find the path to newfound hobbies both exciting and rewarding.

Consider the stories of those who have transformed their lives through new interests. Take, for instance, the retiree who turned a love for pottery into a successful small business, or the individual who discovered a passion for writing and published a memoir. These examples illustrate the transformative power of hobbies. They show how embracing new activities can lead to personal growth, fulfillment, and even unexpected career paths. Such cases inspire us all to view retirement not as an end, but as a beginning—a time to explore, to create, and to cultivate a life rich with passion and purpose.

10.3 Maintaining Health and Wellness

Retirement opens up a world where you can prioritize your health and wellness, giving you the energy and vitality to enjoy this new phase of life. Physical activity plays a crucial role in this, acting as a foundation for sustaining health. Simple routines like daily walks or yoga sessions can have profound effects on both body and mind. A brisk walk in the morning invigorates the senses and sets a positive tone for the day. Yoga, with its gentle stretches and deep breathing, not only enhances flexibility but also calms the mind. Group fitness classes, whether it's water aerobics or tai chi, offer the added benefit of social interaction, connecting you with others who share your commitment to staying active. These activities not only strengthen your muscles and bones but also boost your mood, making you feel more vibrant and engaged with life.

Nutrition is another pillar of well-being in retirement, providing the fuel your body needs to function optimally. Planning nutritious meals with seasonal ingredients ensures you get a variety of vitamins and minerals, supporting overall health. Seasonal produce is often fresher and more flavorful, making healthy eating a delight rather than a chore. Reducing processed foods and sugar intake can have remarkable benefits, such as improved energy levels and better weight management. Consider experimenting with new recipes that emphasize whole grains, lean proteins, and plenty of fruits and vegetables. This approach not only nourishes your body but also allows you to discover new tastes and culinary skills, turning meal preparation into a creative and enjoyable endeavor, now that you have the time to prepare it!

Mental health and emotional well-being are equally important in retirement, providing resilience in the face of life's challenges. Practices like mindfulness meditation and relaxation techniques can support mental clarity and emotional balance. Spending a few minutes each day in quiet reflection, focusing on your breath or a calming image, can reduce stress and enhance your sense of peace. Engaging in activities that promote cognitive health, such as puzzles or learning a new language, keeps your mind sharp and agile. These practices foster a sense of accomplishment and satisfaction, enriching your daily life.

Regular health check-ups and screenings are vital for preventive care, allowing you to address potential health issues before they become serious. Scheduling routine screenings, such as blood pressure checks and cholesterol tests, helps track your health and catch any concerns early. Building a supportive relationship with healthcare providers ensures you receive personalized care tailored to your needs. Open communication with your doctor is crucial; it allows you to discuss any changes in your health and adjust your care plan accordingly. This proactive approach empowers you to take charge of your health, ensuring you remain strong and vibrant throughout your retirement years.

10.4 Traveling on a Budget

Travel is a cherished aspect of retirement, offering new perspectives and enriching experiences. However, ensuring these adventures fit within your financial plan is crucial. One effective strategy is planning trips during off-peak seasons. This not only helps reduce costs significantly but also allows you to enjoy destinations without the bustling crowds. Additionally, utilizing travel rewards and loyalty programs can greatly enhance your travel experience. Many credit cards offer points that can be redeemed for flights or hotel stays, turning everyday expenses into future adventures. Exploring these programs and understanding their benefits can transform the way you travel, allowing you to visit more places without straining your budget.

When it comes to accommodations, thinking outside the box can lead to significant savings. Home exchange programs and vacation rentals provide a comfortable and cost-effective alternative to traditional hotels. Swapping your home with someone in another city or country can give you a local's perspective while saving money. Vacation rentals, such as those found on platforms like Airbnb, often provide more amenities for less cost, especially for longer stays. Another option is staying with friends or family during your travels. This not only cuts lodging costs but also enriches your experience with personal connections. Hosting through Airbnb while you travel can also generate extra income, offsetting your travel expenses.

Exploring local destinations can uncover hidden gems right in your backyard. Often, we overlook the treasures close to home in favor of far-flung adventures. Consider day trips to nearby cultural sites or state parks, which can be both educational and relaxing. Local walking tours or historical visits offer a deeper understanding of your region's history and charm. These smaller excursions require less planning and expense yet can be just as fulfilling as international travel. Embracing local travel helps you appreciate the beauty and culture around you, providing a sense of adventure without the need for extensive planning or expense.

Planning your travels wisely ensures you maximize enjoyment while minimizing costs. Numerous websites and apps offer tools to help you find the best deals on flights, accommodations, and attractions. Websites like Skyscanner and Kayak aggregate deals from various airlines, helping you find the lowest fares. Apps such as TripAdvisor offer reviews and suggestions from fellow travelers, providing insights into must-see attractions and dining options. Joining online communities or forums dedicated to budget travel can connect you with tips and advice from seasoned travelers. These resources empower you to plan trips that are not only cost-effective but also rich in experiences and memories.

10.5 Volunteering and Giving Back

Imagine stepping into a role where your time and skills impact lives in profound ways. Volunteering during retirement not only enriches the community but also enhances your sense of purpose and fulfillment. Engaging in volunteer activities fosters meaningful connections with others and strengthens community ties. The joy of helping someone learn to read or contributing to a local food bank gives life a renewed sense of purpose and satisfaction. Such experiences offer a unique opportunity to leave a legacy of kindness and service, providing both personal gratification and a deeper connection to the world around you.

Finding the right volunteer opportunity starts with aligning your interests and skills with community needs. Local non-profits and community organizations often seek volunteers for various roles, from event planning to mentorship programs. These institutions are a great starting point for those eager to contribute. For those looking for more tailored opportunities, online platforms like VolunteerMatch or Idealist can help connect you with projects that resonate with your passions. Whether you're interested in environmental conservation or supporting education, there are countless ways to make a difference. Identifying roles that match your strengths ensures that your contributions are both rewarding and impactful.

Consider the stories of retirees who have significantly impacted their communities through volunteering. Take, for example, a retiree who devoted time to environmental conservation, planting trees and restoring natural habitats, which not only preserved ecosystems but also inspired others to join the cause. Another retiree found fulfillment in mentoring youth, guiding them through academic challenges and life decisions. These efforts enriched the mentors' lives and opened doors for the younger generation. Such stories illustrate the powerful impact of volunteering, showing how retirees can leave a lasting mark on their communities and themselves.

Engaging in advocacy and activism provides another avenue to make a difference. Participating in advocacy groups or campaigns allows you to champion causes you're passionate about, whether it's environmental issues or social justice. Writing letters or articles raises awareness and encourages others to take action. This involvement not only amplifies your voice but also connects you with like-minded individuals committed to enacting positive change. Through these efforts, you contribute to a better world while finding personal fulfillment in knowing your actions matter.

10.6 Cultivating a Positive Retirement Mindset

Retirement is often seen as a culmination of years of hard work, a time to relish the freedom and opportunities it brings. Embracing an optimistic outlook can transform this phase into a vibrant chapter of life. Start each day by practicing gratitude, acknowledging the small joys and experiences that fill your life. Whether it's the morning sun filtering through your window or a quiet cup of coffee enjoyed at your own pace, these moments remind you of the richness retirement offers. Focus on personal growth and development, setting new goals that excite and challenge you. This time is yours, a reward for the years of dedication and effort. You've worked your whole life to enjoy this time, so allow yourself to explore the possibilities it holds.

In this journey, self-compassion is essential. Be kind and patient with yourself as you adjust to this new rhythm of life. Practice self-affirmations and positive self-talk, reinforcing the belief in your ability to thrive. Allow yourself the time to discover who you are beyond your career, acknowledging that these changes take time. Speak openly with your partner, who may also feel overwhelmed. Sharing your thoughts and feelings can strengthen your bond and provide mutual support, creating a shared understanding of this new chapter. Together, you can explore what retirement means for both of you, finding comfort in each other's company.

Consider the stories of individuals who have embraced a positive retirement mindset, finding joy in unexpected places. One retiree discovered a passion for photography, capturing the beauty in everyday moments, while another found fulfillment in community theater, creating lasting friendships and memories. These stories inspire us to see challenges as opportunities, reminding us that optimism can transform our experience. Embracing this mindset opens doors to new adventures and deeper connections, enriching your life in ways you may never have imagined.

10.7 Embracing Lifelong Learning

Entering retirement opens a world of possibilities for expanding your knowledge. It's an ideal time to explore subjects that pique your curiosity or dive deeper into areas you've always wanted to understand better. Consider enrolling in university courses or adult education programs that cater to your interests. Many institutions offer classes specifically designed for older adults, providing a supportive and engaging learning environment. If attending classes in person isn't feasible, online learning platforms like Coursera or Udemy provide a wide range of topics, from history to technology, that you can explore at your own pace. These platforms offer flexibility, allowing you to learn from the comfort of your home. Engaging in continuous education keeps your mind active and can be immensely fulfilling, offering both personal growth and a sense of accomplishment.

The cognitive benefits of lifelong learning are profound. Studies on neuroplasticity show that the brain continues to adapt and change throughout life, forming new connections and pathways as we learn. This mental stimulation is key to maintaining cognitive health, improving memory, and enhancing focus. Engaging in learning activities challenges your brain, keeping it sharp and resilient. Whether you're solving complex problems in a math class or learning a new language, these activities bolster mental agility. The joy of mastering a new skill or understanding a complex concept brings a sense of achievement that is deeply rewarding. This ongoing mental engagement contributes to overall well-being, providing a sense of purpose and direction.

There is a wealth of resources available to support your educational pursuits. Community colleges often offer a variety of classes and workshops tailored to retirees, providing opportunities to learn new skills or hobbies. Free online lectures and webinars from reputable institutions like Harvard or MIT offer high-quality content accessible to everyone. These resources make it easy to continue your education without the pressure of grades or deadlines. By taking advantage of these opportunities, you can explore new fields and expand your horizons. Whether you're interested in art, science, or philosophy, there's something available that can ignite your passion and satisfy your curiosity.

Consider the stories of those who have transformed their lives through education. One retiree might pursue a degree in environmental science, driven by a lifelong love of nature, while another earns a certification in digital photography, turning a retirement hobby into a small business. Such educational pursuits can lead to personal transformation, opening doors to new adventures and career paths. These stories illustrate the power of learning to enrich your life, offering new perspectives and opportunities for growth. Embracing education in retirement not only enhances your knowledge but also keeps you connected to the world, ensuring that your retirement years are vibrant and fulfilling.

10.8 Celebrating Milestones and Achievements

Recognizing your accomplishments throughout retirement can enrich the experience, turning everyday moments into cherished memories. Consider creating a scrapbook or journal to document these achievements. Whether it's a successful garden yield, a completed painting, or a year of volunteering, each page becomes a testament to your progress and joy. Hosting gatherings for significant events allows you to share these milestones with loved ones, creating a tapestry of shared experiences that weave together the past and present. These gatherings foster connection, reminding you of the support and love that surround you. As you celebrate, reflect on what these achievements mean to you and how they shape your journey forward.

Setting new goals keeps the spirit of growth alive. Vision boarding can be a powerful tool to visualize future aspirations, providing a tangible reminder of the dreams you aim to pursue. Collaborating with your partner to develop goals fosters mutual support, encouraging each other to strive for new heights. Setting and tracking progress toward these goals can transform abstract desires into actionable steps. Whether it's learning a new skill or planning a dream vacation, these aspirations guide your days, infusing them with purpose and anticipation. As you achieve each milestone, the journey becomes richer, imbued with a sense of fulfillment and direction that continues to unfold.

Celebrating these milestones in meaningful ways adds depth to the experience. Planning themed parties or trips to mark special occasions creates memories that linger long after the event ends. Imagine a party themed around a favorite decade or a trip to a location that has always captured your imagination. Hosting a community event to give back can also be a deeply rewarding way to celebrate, turning personal joy into collective benefit. These celebrations not only honor your achievements but also contribute to a broader sense of community and connection. They serve as reminders of the impact you've made and the legacy you continue to build.

Consider the stories of retirees who have celebrated in unique and impactful ways. One might choose to give to charity in honor of a special birthday, transforming personal joy into a gift that touches many lives. Another might commemorate an anniversary by organizing a neighborhood cleanup, celebrating love and commitment through service to the community. These stories inspire us all to find creative expressions of celebration, illustrating how milestones can be marked with intention and generosity. As you celebrate your own achievements, allow these stories to encourage you to think outside the box, finding ways to honor your journey in ways that resonate deeply with your values and aspirations.

10.9 Sharing Your Retirement Journey with Others

Retirement is a time when stories take on new significance, offering a chance to share wisdom and experiences with others. Sharing your journey can build a sense of community and connection, providing support and inspiration. When you share your experiences, you invite others into your world, creating bonds that enrich both your life and theirs. Whether it's a tale of a fulfilling volunteer project or a moment of personal triumph, these stories can inspire those around you. They serve as living legacies, a balance between enjoying the present and leaving something meaningful behind.

There are numerous platforms where you can share your stories. Blogging or vlogging about your retirement experiences allows you to reach a wide audience, offering insights and reflections that may resonate with others on similar paths. Your stories become a source of encouragement, showing that retirement is not an end but a vibrant new chapter. Speaking engagements at local clubs or organizations provide a more personal touch, enabling face-to-face interactions. These venues offer a platform for sharing your journey, sparking conversations and connections that live beyond the initial exchange. By opening up, you create a ripple effect of positivity and inspiration.

Mentorship is another powerful way to share your knowledge. Guiding younger generations or peers entering retirement can be immensely rewarding. Establishing mentorship programs within communities allows you to pass on valuable lessons, providing support and guidance to those navigating similar transitions. Participating in intergenerational exchange initiatives fosters understanding and collaboration, bridging gaps between different life stages. These interactions not only enrich your life but also empower others, instilling confidence and resilience. Your experiences become a beacon, guiding others toward fulfilling and meaningful lives.

Consider the impact of storytelling through examples of retirees who have made a difference by sharing their journeys. Some have become motivational speakers, using their stories to inspire and uplift audiences. Others have used storytelling to impact communities, creating change through shared experiences. These stories demonstrate the power of sharing, illustrating how personal narratives can influence and transform lives. As you share your journey, remember that your story is unique and invaluable, with the potential to inspire and connect in ways you may never have imagined.

Don't move on to the next chapter without doing the following;

1. Have you started planning your next vacation? Go ahead and get planning
2. Have you booked in to start your new hobby or interest?
3. Now you have time how will you improve or maintain your health? Do you need to book something in?
4. Research opportunities for you to volunteer your time and go and visit them
5. Have you planned out your ideal retirement life with a plan and vision board? Get busy planning!

Conclusion

As we reach the end of this guide, let's take a moment to reflect on the journey we've embarked on together. We've traveled through the intricate pathways of retirement planning, covering everything from building a strong financial foundation to exploring the emotional aspects of this life stage. Each chapter has been crafted to offer you insights and practical strategies, empowering you to take charge of your financial future.

Throughout this book, we've tackled essential topics like understanding retirement needs, setting realistic financial goals, and demystifying complex jargon. We've discussed the importance of accelerating savings, making smart investment choices, and navigating the intricacies of Social Security. We've delved into healthcare and long-term care planning, explored the emotional landscape of retirement, and emphasized the significance of estate planning. Finally, we've looked at living a fulfilling retirement, balancing leisure with prudence, and embracing new interests.

Here are some key takeaways to keep in mind as you move forward:

1. **Start Early, Plan Wisely:** Begin your retirement planning journey as soon as possible. If you're starting late, don't despair. Focus on catch-up contributions and smart investment choices to build your nest egg.
2. **Understand Your Needs:** Visualize your ideal retirement and differentiate between needs and wants. Use scenario planning to prepare for unexpected changes.
3. **Diversify Investments:** A well-diversified portfolio can help manage risk and maximize growth. Regularly review your investments to stay aligned with your goals and ensure you do regular check ins on it's performance.

4. **Maximize Social Security:** Timing your Social Security claims wisely can enhance your retirement income. Consider all factors, including health and financial needs, before deciding when to claim.

5. **Plan for Healthcare and Long-Term Care:** Healthcare costs can be significant in retirement. Incorporate these into your financial plans and explore insurance options for added security.

6. **Embrace Emotional Preparedness:** Understand the emotional impact of retirement. Find new purposes and interests to ensure a fulfilling and balanced life.

Now, I urge you to take action. Review the exercises and action steps at the end of each chapter and implement them in your life. Each small step you take brings you closer to a secure and enjoyable retirement. Reflect on your personal situation. How can the lessons learned in this book help you achieve your retirement dreams? Customize the strategies to fit your unique circumstances. Remember, the power to shape your future is in your hands.

As you embark on this new chapter, I want you to feel confident and optimistic. Retirement is not just the end of a career; it is a beginning—a time to explore new passions, make memories, and live life on your terms. You have the tools and knowledge to navigate this transition successfully. Embrace this opportunity with excitement and anticipation.

Before we part ways, let me express my heartfelt gratitude. Thank you for choosing this book as your guide through the complexities of retirement planning. Your trust means the world to me, and I am honored to have been a part of your journey. I hope that the insights and strategies shared here empower you to make informed decisions and lead a financially secure and fulfilling retirement.

Remember, this is your time to shine. The possibilities are endless. With careful planning and thoughtful action, you can create a retirement that resonates with your dreams and aspirations. Here's to a future filled with joy, purpose, and peace.

* * *

Make a Difference with Your Review

People who give without expecting anything in return live happier lives. So, let's make a difference together!

Would you help someone just like you—curious about Financial Freedom but unsure where to start?

My mission is to make Financial Freedom understandable for everyone.

But to reach more people, I need your help.

Most people choose books based on reviews. So, I'm asking you to help someone else by leaving a review.

It costs nothing and takes less than a minute but could change someone's financial journey and turn around a family's future. Your review could help...

...one more family get out of debt
   ...one parent build their emergency fund for their family
   ...one child understand money to start their life out better than they started
   ...one more person take control of their finances
   ...one more dream come true

To make a difference, simply scan the QR code below, or click on the link and leave a review:
   https://amzn.to/4a1Z8DH

Emma Maxwell

References

- *How much do I need to retire? | Fidelity* https://www.fidelity.com/viewpoints/retirement/how-much-do-i-need-to-retire
- *How to Set Retirement Goals: A Guide for a Secure Future* https://www.westernsouthern.com/retirement/how-to-set-retirement-goals
- *Boldin vs Other Best Retirement Planning Software and Tools* https://www.boldin.com/retirement/newretirement-vs-best-retirement-planning/
- *Retirement topics - Catch-up contributions* https://www.irs.gov/retirement-plans/plan-participant-employee/retirement-topics-catch-up-contributions
- *How to Maximize Your 401K Employer Match* https://bankofsunprairie.com/how-to-maximize-your-401k-employer-match.html
- *9 Ways To Make Extra Money in Retirement* https://www.investopedia.com/ways-to-make-extra-money-in-retirement-8716943
- *24 Ways to Cut Costs for Retirement | Boldin* https://www.boldin.com/retirement/20-ways-to-cut-retirement-costs/
- *How to Structure Your Retirement Portfolio* https://www.schwab.com/learn/story/structuring-your-retirement-portfolio
- *Investor questionnaire: Get personalized suggestions* https://investor.vanguard.com/tools-calculators/investor-questionnaire
- *Target-Date Funds: Advantages and Disadvantages* https://www.investopedia.com/articles/retirement/07/life_cycle.asp
- *401k Advice for Employees | Vanguard Institutional* https://institutional.vanguard.com/401k-plans/employee-advice.html
- *How Social Security Benefits Are Calculated* https://www.bankrate.com/retirement/how-social-security-benefits-are-calculated/

- *Retirement Age and Benefit Reduction* https://www.ssa.gov/benefits/retire ment/planner/agereduction.html
- *9 Ways to Boost Your Social Security Benefits* https://www.investopedia.com /articles/retirement/112116/10-social-security-secrets-could-boost-you r-benefits.asp
- *Retirement Income: Required Minimum Distributions* https://www.schwab.c om/learn/story/retirement-income-required-minimum-distributions
- *How has U.S. spending on healthcare changed over time?* https://www.healt hsystemtracker.org/chart-collection/u-s-spending-healthcare-change d-time/
- *When to Enroll in Medicare: Eligibility and Deadlines | Anthem* https://www. anthem.com/medicare/learn-about-medicare/medicare-enrollment#:~: text=The%20General%20Enrollment%20Period%20for,pay%20a%20la te%20enrollment%20penalty.
- *Best Long-Term Care Insurance Companies of 2024* https://www.cnbc.com/ select/best-long-term-care-insurance/
- *How to Plan for Medical Expenses in Retirement* https://www.investopedia.c om/retirement/how-plan-medical-expenses-retirement/
- *Will vs. Trust: What Do You Need? Cost, Process and Uses* https://www.nerdw allet.com/article/investing/estate-planning/will-vs-trust#:~:text=The %20main%20difference%20between%20wills,typically%20must%20go %20through%20probate.
- *Best Practices to Reassess your Beneficiary Designations* https://lumsdencpa. com/blog/view/best-practices-to-reassess-your-beneficiary-designati ons
- *Talking About Estate Planning - Tips from Fidelity* https://www.fidelity.com /life-events/estate-planning/talking-estate-planning
- *10 Common Estate Planning Mistakes to Avoid* https://www.findlaw.com/fo rms/resources/estate-planning/estate-planning-mistakes.html
- *Paying Off Debt in Retirement - InCharge Debt Solutions* https://www.inchar ge.org/debt-relief/paying-debt-after-retirement/
- *7 Smart Ways to Live Well on a Fixed Income* https://seniorhealthcareteam.c om/articles/7-smart-ways-to-live-well-on-a-fixed-income/

- *Retirement Expenses Worksheet* https://investor.vanguard.com/tools-calc ulators/retirement-expenses-worksheet
- *How to Plan for Unexpected Expenses Post-Retirement* https://www.mutual ofomaha.com/advice/be-ready-for-retirement/how-to-plan-for-unex pected-expenses-post-retirement
- *Adjusting to Retirement: Handling Depression and Stress* https://www.helpg uide.org/aging/healthy-aging/adjusting-to-retirement
- *Volunteer Opportunities for Seniors* https://nj211.org/volunteer-opportunit ies-for-seniors
- *Building and Maintaining Social Connections in Retirement* https://atlantics horesliving.com/blog/building-and-maintaining-social-connections-in -retirement/
- *10 Expert Tips On Coping With Retirement Anxiety | StoneRidge* https://www. stoneridgelcs.com/blog/expert-tips-on-coping-with-retirement-anxie ty/
- *Life Expectancy - FastStats* https://www.cdc.gov/nchs/fastats/life-expecta ncy.htm
- *The Best Retirement Planning Apps* https://www.investopedia.com/articles /personal-finance/011916/best-retirementplanning-apps.asp
- *How Inflation Impacts Your Retirement Income - Investopedia* https://www.i nvestopedia.com/articles/retirement/052616/how-inflation-eats-away- your-retirement.asp#:~:text=The%20inflation%20rate%20affects%20 how,financial%20plan%20for%20the%20future.
- *AI To Benefit Humanity: Innovations In Senior Care* https://www.forbes.com /councils/forbestechcouncil/2024/01/30/ai-to-benefit-humanity-innov ations-in-senior-care/
- *50 Inexpensive Hobbies for Retirees - Maus Software* https://maus.com/50-i nexpensive-hobbies-for-retirees/
- *Retirement Hobbies for Better Mental Health | SunLife* https://www.sunlife.c o.uk/articles-guides/your-life/retirement-hobbies-for-better-mental- health/
- *USDA MyPlate Nutrition Information for Older Adults* https://www.myplate. gov/life-stages/older-adults

- *Thrifty Strategies for Senior Travelers* https://www.nytimes.com/2022/09/22/travel/frugal-strategies-for-senior-travelers.html

Also by Emma Maxwell

My first book is a great complement to **Retirement Planning Made Easy**. It sets the fundamentals for saving, budgeting, paying down debts and building an emergency fund - all key enablers to building a retirement nest egg you can securely live on forever. Definitely worth a read!

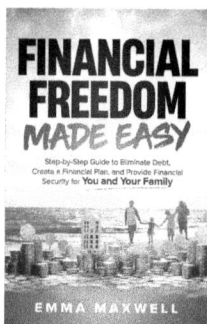

Financial Freedom Made Easy: Step-by-Step Guide to Eliminate Debt, Create a Financial Plan and Provide Security for you and your Family

Achieve Financial Independence and Secure Your Family's Future in Just a Few Simple Steps — Even if You're Starting from Scratch

Financial Freedom Made Easy is your comprehensive, practical guide to financial independence and peace of mind.

Here's just a glimpse of what you'll discover inside:

- **6 practical steps** to create a realistic budget for your family

- The **most effective strategies** for paying off credit card debt, including the *Debt Pay Down* and *Debt Accelerator* methods

- **Emergency Fund 101**: the step-by-step process for building your family's safety net.

- **Investment basics for beginners**: Clear explanations of investing terms and key steps to get you started

- Why **low-risk investment options** can still yield significant returns

- **Easy-to-understand guidelines** for retirement planning to ensure a comfortable future

- **Simple tax planning strategies** to maximize your savings

- How to overcome the **psychological barriers** that hinder good financial habits

- **Real-life success stories** to inspire and motivate your journey

...and so much more!

www.ingramcontent.com/pod-product-compliance
Lightning Source LLC
Chambersburg PA
CBHW071428210326
41597CB00020B/3698